BE INVINCIBLE

5 Steps to Elite Mental Toughness and Relentless Achievement

By Geoffrey Q. Mull

For Tristan and Phillip, whose enthusiasm inspires me.

Contents

Preface

Welcome to the formula for relentless accomplishment in life. You have now set one foot on the path of triumph. This book will outline the concepts, attitudes, methods and techniques used by the world's highest achieving individuals throughout history. If you have a catalyst amount of motivation and desire, following this blueprint will make your achievements not a matter of if, but when.

The majority of failures are the result of flawed strategy and technique, not a lack of effort. Greatness is not inherited or stumbled upon by chance. It is not a fluke and it is not a gift. It is the application of the right efforts in the right places in the right ways. It follows universal methods and common principles - it can be taught, and it can be learned. These principles are intuitive to some, but they are effective for all.

You bring the raw ingredients – a concept and an urge – and we will hone you into an invincible agent of success.

> "We are what we repeatedly do. Excellence, then, is not an act, but a habit."
>
> -Commentary on Aristotle, Will Durant

The 8 Components of Mental Toughness

1. **Emotional Control**: Also called Arousal Control, this is the ability to manage our feelings as they arise, and it includes self-soothing, relaxation/stress management, negative thought control, positive self talk and awareness.

2. **Self Confidence**: This is your mental self-concept. It includes confidence in one's abilities, self-belief, our assessment of our capabilities, strengths and weaknesses, and our evaluations of our efforts. How we perceive ourselves has a strong influence on our actions and how we interact with the environment around us.

3. **Self Control**: Also called self-regulation or willpower. The strength to control our behavior and carry out our decisions.

4. **Concentration**: This allows one to maintain attention and avoid distraction. Also termed Task Focus or Attentional Control.

5. **Visualization**: Examples are imagery control, mental rehearsal and applied experience. Being able to imagine successful efforts and your desired state to create peak performance.

6. **Commitment**: This comprises motivation, desire, and the ability to make self promises and deliver full effort. Being "all in".

7. **Adaptation:** Also termed Resiliency, which is the ability to bounce back from adversity and react productively to unexpected events.

8. **Challenge:** The capacity to see challenges as opportunities instead of threats or obstacles. It is the skill for finding the potential gain in any situation.

The Navy SEALs "Big Four" Mental Skills

1. **Goal Setting**: Maintain focus and combat stress by setting constant short-term goals. (See: Micro Goals)

2. **Mental Rehearsal**: Enhance performance through mental practice runs prior to events. Experience your future success with mental training exercises. (See: Micro Visualization)

3. **Control Self Talk**: By taking charge of the constant dialogue going on it your head, you have the ability to create a positive attitude to achieve more. (See: Positive Self Talk)

4. **Arousal Control**: Use of deliberate breathing to lower the effects of stress and panic to maintain focus and calm. (See: Controlled Breathing)

Step 1: Set the Target - Goals

"Destiny is not a matter of chance, it is a matter of choice;
it is not a thing to be waited for, it is a thing to be
achieved."
-William Jennings Bryan

Mega Goals - Our Roadmaps of Life.

Study after study has shown that people who set goals achieve more. And doesn't this make sense? A goal is a destination, a target, an objective - something to aim our sights at. Without goals, where are we headed, and how will we know when we arrive?

Without goals, we are drifting on the sea of life - like a boat without a rudder. This would make success little more than luck. There is always some element of chance, but successful individuals minimize this effect while maximizing their own abilities of accomplishment. They utilize every element that is under their control to reach their desired ends. And that which is beyond their control they fluidly maneuver. To give accurate direction to these labors we set Mega Goals.

> Mega Goals - our highest level desires and
> achievements in life; the culmination of our striving;
> our life plan; vision of the desired future

These are the long-term ends and objectives that all of our smaller goals lead us towards, our highest ambitions - our ultimate force. Mega Goals reflect our deepest beliefs about what is good in life - our peak aspirations. They are usually somewhat abstract - they likely have to do with family, social and career desires. They are the accomplishments that define our time here on Earth. They build our identity and form our lasting legacy.

Producing Focused Energy

Our Mega Goals reflect our core values and ideals. Their timeframe is typically years or decades. From these our near-term goals will be created as sub-goals of the larger endeavors. Often, before reaching 100% of a goal we still feel a wonderful feeling of accomplishment. This is because while the goal itself is important, its secondary purpose is to provide us with Focused Energy.

> Focused Energy – the ability of an individual to use time and resources effectively to achieve desired outcomes; the efficiency and precision of one's efforts; passion with purpose

This is simply saying that those who use their time wisely and direct it narrowly towards a specific purpose produce greater results – they use their energy with greater efficiency. We have limited resources so we need laser-guided precision for our output.

We know where we are today, and our Mega Goals are where we want to be in the future. The difference between the two produces desire – it is our catalyst to effort, our spur to action, our fuel for change.

In the cloud of emotions, desires, anxieties and confusion that constitute a living breathing human being, it is those individuals who are able to cut through the clutter and put effort into motion with the least distraction and waste who accomplish the most. That is what this book outlines, in concept and in method - making the trip from Point A to Point B the straightest line possible. Staying on that straight path to achievement is made possible by Mental Toughness.

> Mental Toughness - the ability to overcome adversity in pursuit of an objective; the set of traits that enable

one to maintain focused energy to achieve goals;
strength of resolve under stress

Toughness is equated with durability. So we are talking about being able to endure difficulty while staying on task. There are many components to mental toughness. We will discuss these elements individually. They are universal traits that are measurable and applicable to any goal we set. We cannot reach goals without having mental toughness and we cannot have mental toughness without reaching goals - because these traits require practice.

This is what is important to realize at the outset – mental toughness has a specific set of traits or characteristics, but it is fundamentally a mindset – the mindset of invincible achievement – the absolute refusal to quit. And this is a mindset that is built. It has techniques that can be trained and strategies that can be mastered. Mental toughness is learned and perfected through exercise. It is not a personality that one inherits, but a skill-set that anyone can gain.

So, the Mega Goals give us our target and produce focused energy. They pull us like a magnet towards our desired future state. Mental toughness is our ability to maintain that energy and stay on target through any trial.

To clarify the purpose of goals, it is common to think of goals like a finish line – a fixed point across which we pass – an absolute point of reference and a state of being. "I am a college graduate." "I completed a triathlon." "I was on Broadway."

There is another important way to conceptualize goals, more similar to following the tail-lights of a trusted driver in a blizzard, or using the beacon of a lighthouse to orient towards the coast on a foggy evening – a relative point of reference in progress, a mechanism for directional control.

14

What we are talking about here is the goal as a catalyst, the goal as an *action* - the goal's ability to produce Focused Energy.

If success is a spear, at the tip of that spear is the goal.

When billionaire businessman Alexander Spanos turned 70, he set a goal of doubling his net worth in the next 10 years. Why? He is a frugal man. He does not need the money and will notice little lifestyle change from such an increase. But, whether he ends that decade worth y or z, this goal will have provided his life with a fresh tank of Focused Energy. We can see then that goals are not simply desired states or wish lists, but goals also provide:

- Direction, Target, Objective
- Measurement of Progress
- A Sense of Purpose
- A Reason for Sustainable Effort

All this equals Focused Energy which equals accomplishment. Success. Achievement. Now let's go into greater detail as to what an effective goal consists of.

Dare to dream - Challenge Yourself

"Only those who will risk going too far can possibly find out how far one can go."
-T.S. Eliot

The higher you set the bar, the more you achieve. Be realistic, but be optimistic too. Be very optimistic. Don't give yourself an impossible task, but make sure you are challenging yourself – to be effective a goal must be difficult.

This process will increase self-confidence and build momentum like you have never felt before, but you need to muster enough belief in yourself to take the first steps. And you have to make your goals demanding. Remember, you are capable of more than you think. Search your dreams, both present and past – back the whole way to childhood – don't be afraid to think big, very big.

"Carpe diem – seize the day."

Disappointments, school systems, and society all have a way of stifling creativity and enthusiasm as we grow up. In psychology this is called "compromise of aspiration". Don't let it happen. If it has happened, reverse it. Regain your childhood inspiration and ambition. Dream big. What do you *really* want out of life?! Now is your chance to claim it. Stop thinking in terms of limitations and roadblocks; think in terms of triumphs and challenges overcome. Realize that the world truly is your oyster. Be bold.

"Who dares, wins." –Motto of the British SAS

Be Specific, Very Specific

For goals to be effective they must be specific. The more specific the goal, the more focused the energy will be. These are our sights, and we want them dialed in as closely as possible.

"The devil's in the details."

For a goal to be measurable, it must be *specific* and *objective*. If we say, "My goal is to be a fast runner", we have only a subjective basis to evaluate our success. When do you want this to happen? What is "fast"? And for that matter, what distance qualifies you as a "runner"? Such subjective and vague goals have been shown to be less effective and have lower completion rates.

This is why we never want to say simply, "I will do my best." Research has shown this to be a much less effective approach to goal attainment. It's vague, subjective, and all too easy to brush aside.

Remember, our goal is to combat the distraction, confusion and vagueness of life and create conviction and clarity - to create responsibility, accountability, measurement and commitment.

We do this by being specific, objective. Numbers are objective. Put a number to your goal whenever possible. Even if you have to create that number yourself. How many pounds do you want to lose, what marathon time do you want? Dollar amounts, times, pounds, distances, titles, etc. Whatever the unit of measure is in your field of endeavor, use it and be specific.

Be concrete in your time-frames as well. "I will become Mayor someday" or "I will improve my public speaking in the future" is not the type of spur to action we are looking for. Take charge and be definite. Some people set 3 month goals, 6 month goals, 1 year goals, 5 year goals and 20 year goals. You can adjust these later if needed. But the first step to getting what you want is knowing what you want. This includes setting realistic, optimistic time-frames for completion. What exactly do you want, and *when* do you want it?

Think of it as staking your claim, planting your flag. This fixed point will act like a magnet and pull you to action.

Note: If you are having trouble breaking your Mega Goals down into numbers, don't worry about it now. These long-term goals are abstract by nature. We will have opportunities to add objective measurements when we break down into Sub-goals.

Know Yourself

"The most important thing in life is to love what you're doing, because that's the only way you'll ever be really good at it."
-Fred Trump, Father of Donald Trump

The better a driver knows a car, the faster he can drive it. The better an archer knows a bow, the straighter he can shoot it. The better a carpenter knows his tools, the better he can build. The better you know yourself, the more you will accomplish.

Think about yourself objectively. Diagram yourself. Dissect yourself. What are your strengths and weaknesses? What are your preferences, habits, patterns, subconscious fears and hopes? What are you good at, what do you love to do, where and when do you thrive? What makes you tick, what drives you, what stifles you? What is your overall belief about life, your spiritual underpinning? What do you really want out of life?

Are you introverted or extraverted? Outgoing or reserved? Do you like big groups or small gatherings? Numbers or words? What are your hobbies and interests? What fascinates you? What unique experiences do you hold? What specific traits make you unique? What are you capable of?

In business terms, what is your "value proposition", "product offering", "competitive advantage"? Forecast yourself. Predict yourself.

If you were a car, what kind of car would you be? If you were an animal, what kind of animal would you be? If you were cast in a movie, what role would you play? If a company created a position specifically for you, to take advantage of all your best qualities, what position would it be?

Do you tend to be curious or consistent? Risk taking or cautious? Organized or carefree? Agreeable or assertive? Nervous or calm?

Spend 10 minutes in front of a mirror looking yourself in the eyes. What example of a human is it you see? Don't think of the person you wish you were or wish you weren't. Look at the raw material of action, motion, creation and expression standing before you. Quantify it. Strategize it. Understand it. Accept it. Realize your potential. Prepare to unlock it.

If anyone is an expert on you, you know who it should be...

> *Think of 5-10 adjectives or statements about yourself. Write them down.*

Now, use this to start formulating your goals. Don't sell yourself short, but make it a good fit. Tailor the goals specifically to that person in the mirror. An extreme extrovert usually does well in social careers like sales; an extreme introvert usually thrives in academic and artistic endeavors. Effective managers are generally assertive and demanding; excellent counselors commonly show high levels of understanding and compassion. Make your goals a natural fit to your unique talents.

The more closely you align your goals to that breakdown of yourself, the more you will achieve. You have the power to modify these traits, but play to your natural strengths. Give it some thought. Mesh your strongest abilities and aspirations with your highest goals. Put yourself in the ideal environment for success to attain your peak performance.

In 1943, Abraham Maslow called the process of utilizing our full potential for high achievement "self actualization". Research has shown that the efforts leading up to the completion of arduous goals bring us the highest level of satisfaction and happiness. Maslow called these "Peak

Experiences". To reiterate – the maximum positive emotions ("Happiness", "Satisfaction") that psychologists observe in humans are found while we are in a challenging approach to our goals.

In other words, striving for difficult goals that employ our unique talents is the greatest joy we experience in life.

"This above all: To thine own self be true."
-Hamlet Act 1, Scene 3

Dig to the core

Not everyone has a life that is ready to be turned into a movie script. But if you search your deepest motives, you may find more there than you realized. Look under the surface, to see what the real desire or need behind your goal is. What does this goal really mean to you? This is the Core Desire.

> Core Desire – the need or want, on its simplest and most organic level, towards which we strive; root cause; fulfilling our fundamental values

For example, most entrepreneurs don't just want to own a business, they are striving for independence and autonomy. They believe in self-reliance. The goal of a lakeside cabin could be the means, the vehicle, for a grandfather to bond with his grandchildren. That bond is his core desire. He values family connection. The underlying desire of an artist may be to inspire creativity or beauty in others. She values sharing and expression. An athlete may cherish his or her ability to be a role model more than his trophies or fortune. Weight loss could be at the surface of a longing for renewed marital romance, and, believe it or not, some men and women running for political office truly do want to improve the lives of their constituents. Public servants should all ideally have a core belief that we are to use our talents to benefit others.

Thus many goals are a means to satisfying a much deeper, more poignant, need within us. They are a way to affirm our fundamental beliefs about existence. Your goals, and your life, should be an affirmation of your principles, a testament to your belief system – this is the path to happiness and fulfillment.

Core Desires are sometimes more difficult to define then the goals themselves, but they are equally important. Goals that are linked to our deepest values and ideals are more effective and give us greater satisfaction. Our highest goals should be a reflection of the principles that matter most to us. Family, friends, career, our community, our religion, our health, our beliefs – these are typically the elements of our life that define us: our base, our foundation, our nucleus. Our most basic beliefs about what is important in life and what is good.

Define your belief system. Align your long-term goals to the things in life you hold dear. You will perform better and be happier.

Approach it like a toddler. Once you have your Mega Goals in mind say to yourself, "But why?" To that answer say again, "But why?" This will eventually lead you to your Core Desires.

"I want to be a guidance counselor." Why? "I get to work with kids." But why? "Because it is possible to make a positive impact in the life of a child." Why? "Because I want to help people. We should help others."

"I want to start a kennel." But why? "Because I love dogs." Why? "It gives people camaraderie" But why? "Because it gives people a friend. Friendship is important."

Once they're discovered, you may find new ways to fulfill the same Core Desires. You may find that what you thought you wanted to pursue is not what will really give you satisfaction.

The better we understand the connection between our goals and our Core Desires the more potent our Focused Energy becomes. This is why it is important to first know yourself and know what you value in life – it's the key to unlocking your potential. It's the wellspring of motivation.

Dig within yourself until you hit bedrock beliefs, core principles. Build your goals upon this solid ground.

> *Write down 4-5 of your core values and desires. Align them with your Mega Goals.*

Commitment

> "Do or do not, there is no try." –Yoda

For our goals to carry weight, they must be backed by Commitment. You must think of this process as drawing a line in the sand. We are creating a point of no return. We are setting a new course, and we do not plan on looking back.

The Army Ranger school has the unofficial slogan, "Cast or tab." This refers to the mentality that the entering soldier should leave either with a cast from injury or the tab on his shoulder that signifies he has successfully completed the course. Cast or tab – do or die. The absolute refusal to quit. Complete and total commitment.

We will cover many methods to increase and maintain this resolve as you travel along the road to achievement, but your initial act of will is vital to your success. Like the Biblical analogy of the seeds cast on rocky soil that grow up with no roots and are easily led astray, entering into this challenge without adequate commitment makes you little more than a candle in the wind.

This is why people entering substance dependence rehabilitation programs frequently make a pledge of their intentions. As does the President of the United States, doctors, lawyers, law enforcement officers, and others who are about to undertake something requiring great responsibility and dedication.

"I *can* do this. I *will* do this." Attach yourself to your goals with *belief, self-confidence* and *optimism*. Believe that you are capable of achieving. Enumerate the qualities that give you the ability to succeed. Have confidence in those abilities. Feel optimistic as you think of your future success.

Most people are familiar with the term "Self-fulfilling prophecy", which is really synonymous with *expectation*. This is the concept that your belief as to the probable outcome of events influences the actual outcome of events. It's what is called in religious terms "faith", and in psychology jargon "confirmation bias". If you think a certain thing will happen, you interpret all information with that attitude – if you anticipate a negative outcome, you will see negative aspects of the situation. If you anticipate a positive outcome, your mind is more likely to interpret events optimistically. When you dislike someone, you tend to notice the person's faults and not notice the strengths. When you like someone, you tend to see the person's virtues and gloss over their deficiencies. Same person, same actions, but very different perception.

But this isn't just about perception – the point is that your perception changes your actions and therefore actually changes the outcome. You see the person's faults, so you act negatively towards the person, and then the person acts negatively towards you. Your expectation is confirmed.

Likewise, we visualize our success. We believe we will succeed. We are confident we will reach our goals. We expect positive outcome. Hence, we will see the positive aspect of everything we encounter. We radiate optimism. And that optimism will be confirmed by achievement.

This is the power of Commitment. It's a prophecy of success, an act of positive expectation. It fosters accountability and resolve. It is a promise we make to ourselves. It's your life - this is how you take it by the reigns. We are moving to our destiny and burning the bridges behind us.

Once there is no going back, failure is no longer an option.

> *Make a commitment to yourself that you will see these goals through. Feel optimism, self-confidence and belief. Expect success. Make it an oath. Mean it and believe it. Write it down. Say it out loud if it helps: "I commit myself fully to this goal. I can... I will..."*

Case Study: In medieval Scandinavia, Viking warriors developed a ritual that they performed before setting out on a great adventure, such as an attack on a neighboring kingdom or a trading mission at a distant port. They stood up in front of their peer group, raised a cup of mead or beer, and proclaimed a bold oath as to where they would go and what great deeds they would accomplish when they got there. They boasted of the glory and riches with which they would return victorious. They bound this oath to a ring that they wore as a symbol and reminder of their commitment. After making this oath, the warrior would be bound to complete the goal or suffer great humiliation from his countrymen. A strong sense of responsibility, belief and confidence was created by these public rituals of commitment and led to some of history's most impressive accomplishments.

Be Inspirational

Your goal should be a story that will inspire. It has to inspire you, so it should inspire others as well. A great goal will be one that has the ability to make others cry. Emotion acts like a gravitational pull on our will. The stronger a sentiment you have towards your goals, the more deeply you align them with your identity and the story of your life, the stronger that drive will be.

Saving up money to retire to an ocean-side bungalow is a fine and noble goal, but once you start approaching a story that could land you on Oprah or Dateline, now you are on to something.

We aren't superheroes, but we can have heroic motivation and resilience, in whatever endeavor we undertake. Movies are full of these themes: the single mother who works extra jobs to get her kids through college, the paraplegic who learns how to walk again, the soldier who fights tooth and nail to save his buddy behind enemy lines, the cancer survivor, come-from-behinds, come-from-nothings, silencing-doubters, beating-the-odds, underdogs etc. etc.

It is a prominent characteristic of the most poignant achievements that they are concerned with others or an idea beyond ourselves. We certainly admire the self-made millionaire. But it is the stories of self-sacrifice, generosity, loyalty, that strike the hardest note. Think Gandhi. Martin Luther King. William Wallace. Nathan Hale. Mother Theresa.

When we attach our goals to others we multiply our motivation by every person involved. That is why stories of fighting for one's family or one's nation have such power to enthrall. The more we are selfless, the more we strive for a cause, the more inspirational we will be.

Imagine you are thinking back on your life on your 90th birthday and remembering the definitive aspects of your years. Choose what you want these memories to be... Construct your legacy.

Write down your long-term Mega Goals. No one can do this for you.

Examples

Note: These examples are provided to illustrate principles and methods. They are samples of what someone else might do. Do not think of them as absolute or exclusive, but as a reference point to demonstrate the process. Each person is unique, so there is no one "right way". They are not intended to be followed like a blueprint – use them as warm-up tools to jump-start your thinking.

Example 1: Ivy League University

Self-statements: I like reading, writing, researching, understanding, and learning. I am conscientious and patient. I like intellectual interaction. I need contemplation. I dislike mornings.

Core Desire: Education - engage the world around me, make my grandmother proud (family), "The mind is a tool that should not be wasted"; "I owe it to my grandmother to be successful"

Mega Goal: High school junior – Attend Ivy League university

Timeframe: 5 years

Example 2: Army Ranger

Self-statements: I like exercise, being outdoors, martial arts, protecting the weak, patriotism, and travel. I am assertive and authoritarian. I dislike ambiguity. I do well with structure.

Core Desire: Military Success; get out of this town and see the world (explore), have something no one can take away (prove doubters wrong), be part of a brotherhood (friendship), show courage; "It is honorable to serve my country"; "Life should be an adventure"; "I would do anything for those close to me"

Mega Goal: 23 year old day laborer – Pass Army Ranger School

Timeframe: 10 years

Example 3: Business Owner

Self-statements: I like cosmetics, fashion, networking, customer service. I am opinionated and intense. I don't like taking orders. I like enjoying the fruits of my labor.

Core Desire: Self-employment; independence, time flexibility (self-determination), ability to make more money to give 2 daughters a better life (giving others opportunity), have something your daughters can be a part of with you (family time), something to leave them; "I like to be my own boss"; "Making others happy makes me happy"; "Family should do everything together"

Mega Goal: 40 year old customer service representative – Run a Profitable Salon

Timeframe: 10 years

Step 2: Internalize it - Visualize V-Day

> "You must have long-range goals to keep you from being frustrated by short-range failures."
> -Charles Noble

"V-Day" is the term used in World War II for "Victory day". We apply this term to mean the point when we have met a goal – our vision of achievement. We do not want this to be a vague concept in the dreamy, misty future. We want it to be concrete, proximate, and expected – it should feel almost touchable.

Utilize all 5 senses

It has been shown that the more senses we use when we conceptualize, the greater our ability to recall the same concept at a later time. Senses make memory vivid. It stands to reason. We have five senses, and each sense is tied in to different channels in the brain. The more of those senses we use to remember an object, say, a dog, the larger that memory imprint is in our brain.

Suppose I told you I own a dog named Jasper. That would be rather easy to forget. Suppose I told you I named him after my great grandfather Jasper McGee, who was a notorious card shark in New Orleans. I have now created a mental image, a storyboard, and the chances you remember his name have gone up substantially.

Now suppose I described Jasper's appearance. He is a tall, muscular Irish Wolfhound with green eyes and long wiry grey fur. I have now invoked your sense of sight.

In the evening, Jasper enjoys jumping on the couch with whoever is present and lying across our laps as we watch T.V. He enjoys being petted, and his coarse, curly fur feels like a wool sweater as you run your hand across it.

Jasper's bark is a deep, long howl that starts with a guttural rumble and ends in a high, haunting whine. Imagine yourself as the mailman dropping off a package and hearing this primordial threat emanating threateningly from the garage. I have now brought your sense of sound and an emotion of fear into your mind.

Jasper loves water in any form and frequently spends afternoons in the pond below my house chasing toads. When he returns he is soaked with algae-ridden water and mud. He shakes off on the front step and a smell of faint pine needles and moldy leaves lingers for hours. Stubborn as the day is long, he continues to fight losing battles with local skunks, and there is often a sour, pungent note near his bed, even on his driest days.

We will forgo the sense of taste for our example. You now have thoughts of Jasper's sight, smell, sound and feel – as well as a few anecdotal mental images and storyboards. We have created many mnemonics and much depth behind the word "Jasper".

This is a very effective memory tool. Test it. Re-read this chapter in a few days, and see if the word "Jasper", or even "dog", doesn't immediately bring vivid memories to your awareness. That is what we want our vision to be, *vivid*. The longer you dwell on these descriptions, and the more imagination you add to it, the stronger the image will become. This is similar to the phenomenon of meeting someone who tells you, "Oh yes, so-and-so has told me so much about you. I feel like I already know you."

We can make this memory even stronger. On top of using our five senses, we want to add emotions. I could tell you that when I walk Jasper in the evening, I am filled with feelings of pride, and how lonely I was before Jasper arrived. This will intensify your mental picture of Jasper significantly and increase your recall ability.

Emotions have exceptional memory-creating power. Who doesn't remember where he or she was when the September 11th bombing struck? We remember precise details of this day, and this is because of the strong emotions attached to it. Similarly, think back on broken bones and broken hearts in your life, these high-emotion type events always carry with them very vivid memories. "Feels like it was just yesterday." This phrase is used for the memories attached with poignant emotions, and those emotionally-heavy memories shape our future behavior.

This is what we will do with V-Day, our mental image of the achievement of our goal. We will turn it into a vivid, realistic narrative to pull our behavior towards our desired future.

Imagine that moment of triumph. Put as many senses and emotions to it as you can. Dwell on each one and commit it to memory. Build in a story around it. Our brains are programmed to use stories to codify information. Draw in people likely to be present, surroundings and feelings. Where will it take place? What things will you see? What things will you touch, what will they feel like? What will you smell, what sensations will go through your body? What will you say, what will your expression be? Will you be out of breath, will you be drinking a toast? What will those things taste like?

Day dream. Again, invoke all your sensory inputs. Walk through it in your mind. Imagine it. Savor it. Simulate it in every way you can - how others may react to the news, how you will tell them, how you might smile or laugh, the reward or rest you may give yourself, any symbols of your success that will be present, and the feeling of accomplishment you will have. Name the specific emotions you will feel that moment.

Note: Resist the temptation to rely too heavily on the reactions or accolades of others. Since humans are difficult creatures to predict by nature, spending too much effort building images of what they may or may not do at a certain time is a recipe for disappointment. Concentrate more on your own reactions and experience of your success. Mentally tough individuals are self-motivated.

Put everything together that will exist in that moment of reality. This will become your beacon, your guiding light in the darkness of the struggle. Visualize your success - see it as real and probable. Begin to look forward to it. This is how we build belief and strengthen commitment.

"Keep your eyes on the prize."

The stronger you make this image, the more senses and memories you attach to V-Day, the easier it will be to bring that image up when you need to refocus, redirect, and reaffirm your resolve. Make it vivid; make it real. These images enhance and bind our Focused Energy. They solidify our belief and optimism, which is a strong predictor of eventual success.

> *Spend some time thinking about your V-Day. Write it down with as much description and as many senses as possible. Add emotions. Use adjectives. Create a small movie that you can watch in your head telling the story of your day of triumph, with you as the main character.*

The V-Day image is a bulwark of mental toughness. It is a constant reminder of why you are striving. Your goals will change from something vague and distant to something real and tangible. It will give you your first taste of success.

Create A V-Day Symbol

When we are back in the day-to-day struggles of life, often feeling like we are in the eye of a tornado, we need to be able to keep our V-Day images in our mind. Remember, our goals provide direction and consolidate our efforts. And our V-Day images are a way to keep those goals close by.

However, the effort and time it takes to go through our entire V-Day simulation is often prohibitive. We become too overwhelmed, stressed, or just plain exhausted to go through that process. We need a shortcut. Therefore, we create a V-Day Symbol.

> V-Day Symbol – a still-frame image that encapsulates all the senses and emotions of reaching your goal in one, instantaneous thought

This could be anything, but will most likely be the object or scene you identify as the principle symbol of your achievement. For a speed skater training for the Olympics the V-Day Symbol would probably be the gold medal. (It could also be a static image of the skater standing on the podium with the medal around his or her neck.) It could be your college acceptance letter, the clock at the finish line of a marathon with a certain time on it, or the sign hanging above the doors of your non-profit organization. Anything that stands out as a fundamental element of your V-Day image is a potential symbol.

When the skater is yet months away from the competition, in the middle of a strenuous conditioning session, or while rehabilitating an injury, he or she may have a moment of doubt or feel pessimism creeping in – at this moment the V-Day Symbol will be quickly brought to mind, the image of that shining, gleaming gold medal, and as all the emotions and motivations surrounding that symbol flood to mind, a renewed sense of Focused Energy will appear to spur the athlete on. The V-Day Symbol is used to bolster mental toughness and refocus in moments of duress. It's an instant injection of motivation.

In the face of rejection and disillusion an actor will pull to mind the vision of the Oscar. During long practice sessions a race car driver will imagine the bottle of milk at victory lane. An exhausted mother imagines her son grown up and successful as she makes his lunch in the pre-dawn hours.

Whatever strong image you want to invoke, use it and stack all the other V-Day memories behind it. You will be recalling this one image often. It is your quick link to all the emotions, hopes and dreams that you carry with you every second of every day, but are often too busy and beleaguered to concentrate on. Like the way a wedding band symbolizes an entire marriage, or a flag symbolizes the history and spirit of a nation.

This is the carrot we chase. When we feel like we are sinking in quicksand, we throw our lasso around this V-Day Symbol and use it to pull ourselves back on dry land. We keep it as a magnet pulling us forward. It is a life-preserver and safety harness, as well as fuel for our internal fire and food for our will power.

Decide on a V-Day Symbol for your goals. Write it down. Visualize it. Associate it with your efforts.

Examples

Example 1: Ivy League College

Visualization: Graduation – It's a warm day in late May. As I walk across the platform to shake hands with the school president, I have to pull up my gown so that I don't trip. As my name is called, I hear my grandmother clap and whistle. I smile as I grip the diploma and walk down the other side of the stage. "Wow, I didn't think I would be so nervous." My palms are sweaty. Finally, the procession starts out to the sound of the alma mater being played by the band. "Wow, I did it! I'm a college graduate." Huge hugs to friends and promises to keep in touch. Under my gown is the faded sweatshirt with the college logo on it that I bought as a freshman. It's too hot so I take it off. Meet up with family and a few friends to eat dinner and celebrate. The cool iced tea is a godsend after those 3 hours of standing. We make jokes about the commencement speech and some of the more vocal parents...

V-Day Symbol: graduation gown and hat; or sweatshirt with school logo on it

Example 2: Airborne Ranger

Visualization: Home on Leave – As you board your flight home and stow your duffle bag on the overhead storage, you can't believe it's over. What an experience that was! Harder than you had expected, but definitely worth it. "I'm a Ranger now." Wow. As the plane lands, you adjust your beret. It feels like everyone in the airport is staring at you as you walk through the terminal. You feel proud. You are now part of the elite. You look down at your Ranger Tab. There's so much still to come. You look up and see your folks waiting for you. Smiles and hugs all around. They seem to look at your differently now, especially your little brother. After a nice dinner and a hot shower, you hang your uniform up. It looks nice, smart, important. Sharp. You find a pair of jeans and a t-shirt and meet some local buddies for a beer. Wow, this beer tastes great. It's the first one you've had in months. You think about how many gallons you sweated since last time you saw these guys. The air conditioning feels great. They give you some gentle ribbing about being a lethal weapon who might kill them by accident, you play a couple of your favorite country songs, everything feels right in the world...

V-Day Symbol: Ranger Tab on your shoulder; or beret

Example 3: Start a Business

Visualization: Opening Day – 6 A.M. and the alarm goes off. Not that you needed it, you barely slept a wink last night. Too much excitement. All those months of work, and it's finally here. Today you are officially a business owner! In 2 hours you will be opening – what a memorable day this will be. A quick breakfast, you pick up an extra large coffee and one for each of your four new employees. You want them to be on their top game as well. You wave hello to a fellow business owner in an adjacent building as you open your doors. Turn on the lights, start the registers. Everything is in place, it looks perfect. The smell of fresh paint and carpets is better than a new car. To you it smells like freedom. Your employees show up right on time and seem as eager to hit the ground running as you are. Your radio ads have been running for a week so you expect an immediate flux of sales. It's a great jumpstart that you already have some appointments lined up. You glance over your sales targets for a quick second before its time to officially open the doors. So far, so good. The customer service skills you have drilled into your staff are working well. They have a few questions here and there, and you service some of the customers yourself to set the tone, but overall its going well. You drive to pick up a quick lunch of sandwiches for the crew and get another coffee for yourself. Sales are solid for a first day! Your mentor stops near day's end to say hello. It feels good to make money, and the independence is motivating. You lock up, and look at the sign above your head. Hard to believe it's real. It's an attractive logo. Very professional. As you drive home, you put on the radio and sing along with a newfound feeling of triumph. You'll take a quick shower, change, get dinner for the kids, make some quick notes for tomorrow, and relax to an episode of Criminal Minds...

V-Day Symbol: Business sign; or Image of Store Showroom

Step 3: Break it Down - Building Blocks of Triumph

"Self-confidence is the first requisite to great undertakings."
-Samuel Johnson

Alright, so we now have our goals in mind, we understand ourselves and our deepest motivations in life, we have created a strong vision surrounding what our day of victory will be like, and have a symbol that summarizes all of this is a quick, easy-to-access and effective way.

Now it's time to break this vision down into actionable items. We are creating a systematic blueprint for success – the roadmap to your future - an action plan for unstoppable achievement.

Sub-goals

"How do you eat an elephant? One bite at a time."

The human mind is an amazing instrument. But it does have limitations. When we try to take on too much at one time, we feel overwhelmed and daunted. When faced with an enormous project it is not uncommon to sink into a feeling of over-arching dread. Like a computer crashing during a program that requires mammoth processing speed, we are simply over-taxing our coping abilities – system overload.

If we take a brilliant lawyer out of his office, put him on a plot of land and tell him to build us a house, he will have no idea where to start. He may even have a panic attack. The project is too big for him to think about as a whole.

 If we take a seasoned contractor and do the same thing, he will immediately get to work – he will draw out a sequence for the process from start-to-finish with accompanying time-frames, and then contact architects, excavators, masons, carpenters and all the other necessary components of the undertaking. He will be able to tell us throughout the process whether he is ahead of schedule or behind. And he will feel comfortable and confident. He knows exactly where to start.

The lawyer is out of his element. He doesn't have the knowledge or experience at this time to complete the goal, and isn't even sure how to start. He can't tackle such a large task all at once - it will only overwhelm him. Pessimism will set in, his confidence will falter, and he will lose his Focused Energy.

He can accomplish this task. But first he will have to step-back, plan, prioritize and learn about house-building. Like all large endeavors this is something one must chip away at. He will cut it up into small, easy to chew, easy to digest pieces. These are our Sub-Goals.

> **Sub-Goals**: Short-term goals that are increments, components, building-blocks of our Mega Goals; stepping-stones on the way to higher accomplishments

For some Mega Goals, the Sub Goals are obvious. Someone who wants to be president will first aim for becoming a Senator or Governor. Someone who wants to be a Karate black belt will want to first become a yellow belt. Likewise, someone who wants to become an accountant will first have to learn tax codes and finance.

We break down those huge goals into smaller goals, and the longer term goals into shorter term goals. This keeps our attention in the present, on the immediate task at hand. Humans are inevitably near-sighted in our thinking. Rather than fight this we exploit it. The sooner and smaller a goal is, the easier it is to accomplish.

Keep breaking down your Mega Goals into yearly, monthly, weekly or daily Sub Goals. It's not as difficult or time consuming as it may sound. You want to end up with specific tasks for short-term action. The point is to know exactly what you need to do in the near-term to gain what you want in the long term. Once you get to the level of specific actions, you are good to go. When the goals turn into individual tasks, it's time to stop planning and start doing.

We keep goals small enough to maintain our Focused Energy and stay motivated. This is a theme we will return to in part four, Adapt and Conquer. But first let's provide some systems for thinking about and planning Sub-Goals, our stepping-stones of achievement.

Note: It is often helpful in our beginning Sub-Goals and Milestones to concentrate on behavior metrics rather than units of measure. For instance, for weight loss we might set goals of frequency and time spent in the gym rather than pounds lost. This allows us to set the groundwork in habits and avoids us losing motivation before our mind and body becomes acclimated to the new routine. Because beginning progress is often small and then builds momentum, it helps to put your early attention on your actions and activities rather than outcome.

Milestones

"Even the tallest mountain has steppes."
-Afghan Proverb

Some of your Sub Goals will be components needed for your success, such as learning skills and honing techniques. And some of them will be marked as Milestones along the path of accomplishment.

Suppose your Mega Goal is to become a NASCAR champion. Along the way you will work your way up through go kart circuits, sprint car championships, and lower level local and regional stock car organizations. Each one of these steps will be considered a Milestone.

Milestones – definite increments leading closer to greater goals; sequential achievements

Likewise, imagine you want to run a 6 minute mile. Your current level, or baseline, is 9 minutes. Cutting a full third off your time is quite a hill to climb. It's a daunting proposition. But taking 30 seconds off your time seems well within reason. So our first Milestone is 8:30. Then 8:00, 7:30, 7:00, and so on. If you experience difficulty, change the Milestones. 15 seconds is still a great barometer of progress.

As before, we want to set specific target time-frames for our Milestones so we can measure our progress. Use objective numbers as much as possible. These goals are typically much more measurable than the Mega Goals. For the above example, our time-frame for each 30 second increment could be 14, 30 or 60 days.

We are setting up a string of checkpoints along the path of triumph – tiers of success. We are building momentum.

Write down the logical Milestones that will lead you to your Mega Goals. Create the big picture by numbering them in sequence or creating a chart.

Nascar Driver:

Go Kart ⟹ Sprint Car ⟹ Local Stock Car ⟹ Regional Stock Car ⟹ NASCAR

1. Go Kart Champion
2. Sprint Car Champion
3. Local Stock Car Champion
4. Regional Stock Car Champion

5. NASCAR Champion

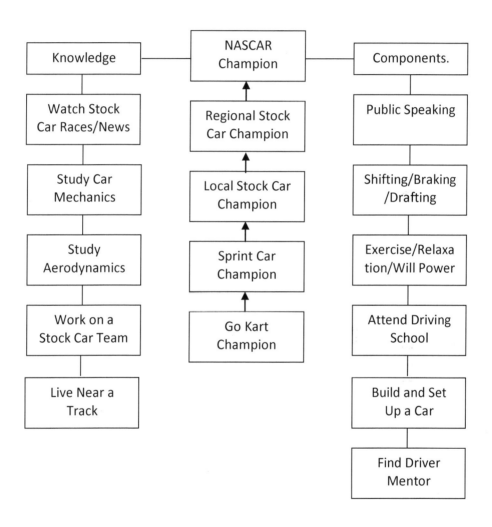

Tasks

To make progress, we need action. Tasks are the individual actions or behaviors we do in the short-term to reach goals in the longer-term. If you goal is to be wearing shoes, the tasks are locating shoes, putting on socks, slipping on shoes and tying shoes. Because tasks require action, they begin with verbs.

We will continue to break down our Sub Goals and Milestones until they become individual, short term tasks. These are the smallest components and the easiest to measure. When your plan gets to this level of detail, it is ready to execute.

> *Write a list of the common tasks you will perform to reach your goal.*

Knowledge

> "Knowledge is the father of efficiency. Efficiency is the shortcut to success."

Learn as much as you can about the field surrounding your goal. Become an expert. If you want to become a supermodel, start studying fashion and makeup. Research hair products and styling techniques. Learn the history, the lore, the movers and shakers, the brands and designers. Subscribe to trade journals and magazines. Read books. If there are classes in your field, take them. If there is a club of people interested in it, join. If there are T.V. shows or movies about it, watch them. Know as much as possible. Saturate yourself in knowledge surrounding your goal.

Don't "learn the hard way". Avoid "rookie mistakes". A little preparation saves a lot of perspiration. And preparation builds confidence. The more you know, the better equipped you are; the more realistic your expectations will be. You will make fewer missteps, suffer fewer frustrations, and in the end make faster progress.

Some examples: Classes, research, T.V., films, magazines, clubs, books, newsfeeds

> *How can you become an expert in the areas surrounding your goal? Write down as many ways as you can think of.*

Components/Skills

Many endeavors have specific skills that are used repetitiously – baseball players have a swing, financial analysts use Excel, lawyers speak in public, pilots navigate. If you can break down your goals and find out the specific skills you will be using to reach them, then you can improve these skills as individual components. Find ways to practice these elements. Increase your skill set in the small areas that assemble into overall mastery.

> *What skills can you master that will increase your effectiveness? What can you become good at that will help you achieve your goal? Write down as many as you can.*

Case Study: Researchers Proffitt, Witt, Linkenauger, and Bakdash did an experiment in which participants practiced putting at distances of either 7 feet or 1.5 feet. They then sat beside the hole and estimated its size. Those who practiced the easy putt estimated the size of the hole to be smaller than those who practiced at the greater distance. Practicing small, easy components builds our skill, confidence and belief for larger endeavors.

Universal Skill I: Controlled Breathing

Stress is a universal aspect of human existence. It's unavoidable. And while its parasitic effect on length of life and psychological health is well-proven, it does have the benefit – with the correct measure and approach – of spurring us to action. Who hasn't seen a boss who gets the most out of his employees by "lighting a fire under them", in other words creating stress to increase their output?

So, when controlled, we can use stress to maintain motivation and increase output. But, left unchecked, stress, and the panic it creates, erodes our quality of life and our productivity. Cortisol, the stress hormone, has been linked to just about every disease and aging process there is. So regardless of our particular goals, every person alive will benefit from the ability to manage stress levels.

Under stress, the amygdala region of the brain is activated and panic begins. Being able to remain cool headed when anxiety is thrown at us allows us to maintain our Focused Energy and not get pulled off the straight path from Point A to Point B. It also increases our ability to make good decisions. Elite snipers and counter-terrorist soldiers such as Delta Force actually hook their bodies up to physiological monitoring (biofeedback) machines and with the help of psychologists learn to control their breathing and heart rate in order to remain calm and stress-free under the intense strain of battle. It keeps them healthy and makes them efficient. This skill is just as applicable to your goals.

Arousal regulation, also called emotional control, is a cornerstone of mental toughness. It has been demonstrated that this skill can be heightened through relaxation training. The most basic way to achieve arousal control is through controlled breathing.

Therefore we recommend everyone, whether you are preparing for the Olympics, losing weight, climbing the corporate ladder or studying to become an R.N., learn and perfect relaxation techniques.

There are many good breathing relaxation techniques available. Explore them and find one you like. Here is a simple method to begin practice:

> *Inhale slowly and deeply through your nose while counting to five, hold the breath for two, then exhale fully for another five count. As you breathe in, use your whole diaphragm and feel your belly button rise as you fill your lungs. Repeat 3-5 times. Next, tense the muscles of you feet and lower legs. Hold for 3 second, and release. Repeat this process along with the slow breathing. Work your way up your body, tensing and relaxing your legs, abdomen, upper body, arms, neck, and face. Continue breathing cycle for 2-3 minutes.*

This could be considered the "long form". Here is a shortened version taught to Navy SEALs that can be used in the heat of the moment – be that the battlefield, before a presentation, walking into a sports arena, or before initiating contact with a member of the opposite sex:

> *Inhale slowly and deeply counting to six. Hold for two seconds. Exhale slowly and fully counting to six. Repeat until calm.*

Note: Avoid short, shallow breathing. Use your whole diaphragm. Maximize the volume of your lungs to gain valuable oxygen. Relax your stomach muscles and feel the air push your belly button out as your lungs expand fully.

In time your relaxation will become quicker and more automatic. You will quickly be able to return to a state of calm at the onset of stress. Feel your heart rate stabilize as you regain your center. Stay calm, stay focused, and stay on task.

Practice relaxation techniques 5-10 minutes per day for two weeks or until they become automatic. Use as needed to maintain a calm, productive state of mind.

Universal Skill II: Forge Iron Will

"The gem cannot be polished without friction, nor man perfected without trials."
-Chinese Proverb

It has been shown that self-control (will power, self-regulation) is a greater predictor of success in individuals than I.Q, peer evaluation, academic performance or SAT scores. Psychologists are able to measure, and train, will power in children as young as kindergarten. It is applicable for all goals, and can be improved through practice.

Self-control is not a "born with" trait. It is an attribute that can be exercised and improved. Think of it as your brain's muscles. Like all muscles it needs to be worked out.

Will power is a foundation for all human accomplishment. It is a building block for all our efforts. It is fuel for the achievement engine. It is a keystone of mental toughness.

While the entire process of striving for goals is an organic self-control booster, all individuals will find it beneficial to practice will power enhancing techniques separately. This is part of the concept behind the yearly Lenten fasts many Christians make – we build up our stores of will power in small things so they are available to use for big things. We aim to discipline the mind the same way an athlete disciplines the body.

Effective techniques to build self-control can be anything that causes a conscious deviation from your normal routine. A few examples are dietary restrictions such as no salt or soda, or only watching a set amount of T.V. per day. These are negative techniques, in the sense that they take something away – you are "giving up" or omitting something.

A challenge that almost everyone can utilize is annoyance control. We all have someone or something that annoys us to death – an in-law, co-worker, friend's slobbery pet, traffic – instead of letting this daily thorn cause you un-needed stress, try controlling the annoyance and use it as a tool to hone your mental discipline. A win-win situation – lower your stress levels and increase your mental strength.

There are also positive techniques in which something new is added, such as following an exercise program, bicycling instead of driving to work, eating a vegetable at every meal, or wearing a tie to work every day. (The last one was used by Mark Zuckerberg, founder of Facebook, for an entire year. He sets a new such goal every year.)

Sticking to an exercise plan has been shown to increase self-control that transfers into all areas of life. Exercise is the premier mental toughness booster. It is the perfect way to "hone the blade" – an arena to practice the techniques of mental discipline that will carry you to triumph. For this reason everyone should follow some exercise regimen, whether or not it is part of specific goals.

"Steel sharpens steel."

The point is to take yourself into deep waters. Shock your system. Put yourself under stress and practice your response. Think of it like a flight simulator. Learn your mental and physical reactions. Self-control in small tasks transfers into self-control in large tasks. This is practice where failure or success is not mission-critical. A slip-up here is less costly then a slip-up while directly pursing your goals. Hone the blade of self-regulation, reset your limitations and see for yourself you can do much more than you thought.

Begin an exercise plan. Write down at least one additional self-control-building technique that you can begin immediately. As always, be specific. Track your progress.

Universal Skill III: Internal Locus of Control

"Great spirits have always encountered violent opposition
from mediocre minds."
-Albert Einstein

Locus means "place" or "position". Locus of Control refers to whether a person feels that the control of his or her life lies internally or externally. What is the source of what happens to you in life? Is the prime influence from inside or outside? Is it what you do, or what is done to you? Is your life, your circumstances, and your success largely controlled by external forces, or does the responsibility for how things turn out lie predominantly within you?

A person with an Internal Locus of Control is likely to feel personally capable to change circumstances to fit his or her desires. This person is proactive, hopeful, practical, and opportunity-focused.

A person with an External Locus of Control feels subject to the whims of others – a helpless victim of Fate. This person is passive, and prone to Vacuum Thinking.

Vacuum Thinking – dwelling on the negative, or empty, aspect of situations; being happy only with the ideal instead of the practical; concentrating on obstacles instead of solutions, seeing barriers instead of opportunities; finding excuses, blaming

Vacuum Thinking is just that – a vacuum, a black hole that sucks you in. It doesn't get you any closer to your achievements, and it wastes time. It is the enemy to adaptation. This is a defeatist attitude. It is lamenting the sale you didn't make or the pass you didn't catch. To achieve you must be forward-thinking and an obstacle must be just that – something to overcome.

The opposite of this is Opportunity Thinking, looking for the positive aspect of a situation – taking responsibility. This is finding the proverbial "silver lining" in the cloud, "making the best of it". The focus is what you do have, not what you do not have – on what you can do, not on what you cannot.

Someone with an Internal Locus of Control is not swayed easily by the actions, words or opinions of others. This person does not let the world get him or her down. It is the belief that an individual can make a difference and that you alone are the master of your destiny. Yes, things will happen to you that you cannot prevent. But what you always, always control is your reaction.

We will elaborate on this idea in Step 4, but what we want to begin cultivating here is the attitude – you control your ultimate destiny. You decide your future. You set the path. Winds may blow and trees may fall across that path, but the decisive control - the critical power – always remains in your hands.

The words of others are rain drops that roll off. You must have an internal truth. You cannot govern what they say, but you always decide how you let it affect you. There is no situation in which you do not have an element of control. If a school rejects your application, you can reapply. Spend a year in community college. Or apply to a better school. Instead of blaming the school you can rewrite your essays, increase your SAT scores, and add some extracurricular activities. You take charge, and "lift yourself up by your boot straps".

This is the mindset of the mentally tough - the rugged individualist. They don't let outside forces get them down. Disappointment lasts only a minute, and then they are planning the next step forward. Your victory is within your grasp, and no one else's.

In every challenge you encounter, avoid Vacuum Thinking. Concentrate on what you have within your power to change. Write down an obstacle you currently face, and how you will take personal responsibility and direct problem-solving action in the situation.

Support Mechanisms – Helpers, Role Models and Mentors

"No man is an island." –John Donne

Don't be afraid to rely on others to help you reach your goals. It is common in substance abuse counseling to have the client inform his friends and family of his intention to kick the habit. This accomplishes two things: it gives the substance abuser a feeling of responsibility and brings his associates on board as support and assistance.

If a loved one can help you stay motivated along your quest, you should take advantage of that. Any increase in your Focused Energy is welcome, internal or external. Never be too prideful to pull other people around you to add to your support system. Elite military units function in family-like squads, politicians have a staff, athletes have coaches and teammates, CEOs have VPs – the point is you should not feel the need to accomplish your goals on your own. Get energy from those around you. Healthy, strong, mentally tough individuals are those who know how to rely on others to increase their effectiveness.

If you can find a mentor in a related field, or someone who has already accomplished what you have set out to do, ask him or her to mentor you. Most people are more than happy to pass on their knowledge and find it a pleasure to do so. A good mentor will help you maintain your inspiration, help you to avoid common pitfalls, and offer camaraderie and commiseration unparalleled by anyone outside your field. After all, "If she did it, so can I."

> "He that walks with wise men shall be wise."
> -Proverbs 13:20

If you can find a partner pursing a similar goal, team up and strive together. Think of her or him as your "battle buddy". It is common for people to have running partners and lifting partners. They motivate each another, provide emotional balance, advice and friendly competition. If you can find someone, buddy up and use your consolidated strengths to form a synergistic alliance. Life's experiences are always more enjoyable when shared with another person.

Jeremy Deeble, a world-famous network marketer, started his empire with the simple premise: "If you want what successful people have, do what successful people do." He went out and found the highest-achieving network marketers he could, asked them to mentor him, and mimicked his way up to the top. He has become an innovator in his own right, but it was a climb that he started on the backs of his mentors and role models.

If you have trouble finding a mentor or battle buddy to interact with directly, look for a role model. Learn about your role model. Mimic the successful habits of this person. Make this person the standard by which you judge yourself. It will inspire you and increase your belief in the possibility of accomplishing your goal. Feeling yourself follow in the footsteps of a highly accomplished individual can do wonders for our optimism and self confidence.

Write a list of prospective support mechanisms from your family and social circles. Search for mentors, battle buddies and role models related to your specific goals. Inform them of your goals and ask them to support you. Begin building your support system.

Don't take on too much

If, once you finish this chapter, you look over your notes and they are several pages long – or if looking at them makes you feel overwhelmed – fall back and regroup.

This has to feel manageable. Don't get bogged down. A good plan is simple to understand, simple to explain, and simple to carry out. Not easy, but simple.

Prioritize. Concentrate on the bigger tasks first. Starting with the items you deem least important, begin crossing things out until you feel comfortable and confident again. Be able to "wrap your head around it" with relative ease while maintaining the element of challenge.

A mentor can be a huge help in this process. An experienced veteran will know what is realistic/pertinent and can help you whittle your notes down for maximum efficiency. Becoming an expert in your area of interest will also help you aim your efforts and prioritize your actions.

Contingency Planning - Head Distractions off at the Pass

Part of knowing yourself is understanding the types of distractions you frequently encounter. Know your weaknesses. Imagine the turbulence you are likely to encounter as you progress towards your achievements – family obligations, social resistance, stress from work, delays, rejections – each and every roadblock and hiccup that can knock you off course or delay your progress.

The better we can foresee and forestall these daily parasites of productivity, the more progress we will make. What has kept you from reaching goals in the past? What situations are you likely to encounter that are out of your control? What do you think will be the most difficult part of your undertaking? Where do other people often drop off the path?

> *Write down the distractions you are most likely to experience during your efforts. Be prepared for them.*

If we plan for these contingencies effectively beforehand, we disarm them, take away some of their sting, reduce their element of surprise, and minimize their impact on our Focused Energy. It is always easier to deal with the expected then the unexpected. So even if you find that there is no way to avoid a specific disruption, the simple fact that you are prepared for it mentally will increase your success.

First Step

> "The future depends on what we do in the present."
> -Mahatma Ghandi

Saying we should plan our initial entry method towards our goals seems simple-minded. But its importance is highly under-rated. Just like rolling a wheel barrow along the ground, it's the initial motion that takes the most effort.

Where do you start? The first step may be the hardest. This is often the movement we don't make, and it's a surefire way not to achieve. As we progress we continue to build momentum and much focus will be on simply keeping the train on the tracks. Many people fail just because they don't start. Clearly indentifying your First Step will make sure you start the race.

Write down the First Step you will take towards your goals. Think small. Be specific. Include a time-frame.

Goal Journal - Treasure what you Measure

It's a proven fact that our consciousness increases when we keep tabs on something. Any businessman worth his salt tracks his daily sales and expenses, and knows exactly where he stands at any given point. Likewise, if a manager wants to get the most out of his or her employees, they are instructed to document their work in a given area and make a report of it at set intervals. If we have to spend the effort to track something, we subconsciously know it must be important.

How many tires did each mechanic change today? How many phone calls did each telemarketer make? How many rebounds did the forwards get? How much can you bench press? How big are your biceps? What's your net worth?

Yes, we "treasure what we measure". We track the things we value. Consistently documenting progress keeps our goals in the forefront of our minds, aids us in seeing and celebrating our success, renews our resolve, keeps our momentum under pressure, and in general helps us maintain our Focused Energy.

It is a common downfall that we look more at how far we have to go than at how far we have already come. Keeping a detailed log of our efforts combats this and keeps us concentrated on the task at hand.

Start a goal journal. Get a notebook or start a Word document to record your goals and log your progress.

Update it on a regular basis. Use a calendar if it helps.

Examples

Note: Sub Goals and Milestones should be broken down until you feel comfortable with them as useful short-term tasks. This will usually be once they reach a weekly or daily focus.

Example 1: Ivy League University

Sub Goals
Get GPA in top 5% of class every term junior and senior year
Maintain a 95% average in all classes every week
Letter in a varsity sport (junior and senior years)
Have 3 extracurricular activities or clubs, be an officer in 1 of them (every year)
Get SAT score in the top 10% nationally by end of junior year
Procure 3 excellent recommendations from impressive people by October of senior year
Write admission essays by October of senior year and have them qualified as excellent by your English teacher
Get into a national honor society by end of junior year

Year 1 Action Plan
Goals: Visit 4 schools; recruit recommendation writers; complete 4 rough drafts of admission essays; acceptant to honor society; letter in varsity sport; have GPA in top 5%; decide on top 5 schools to apply to.

Month 1 Action Plan
Goals: Join 3 clubs; join varsity sports team; identify a national honor society and get application; learn admission process and metrics.

Week 1 Action Plan

Goals: Begin exercise program with 3 workouts; ask teacher to be mentor; get SAT book and start studying; get 95% in all exams.

Tasks
Study for classes
Attend extracurricular meetings
Practice SAT
Recruit recommendations
Write admission essays
Apply to honor society

Knowledge
Learn the metrics for the college admission process of top schools
Learn the ranking metrics of colleges and what the top ranking schools are
Learn about the sport you are playing and possible fields of study (your major)
Learn about the SAT, how it is administered, how it is scored

Skills/Components
Increase vocabulary, math and writing skills by end of junior year
Master the curriculum of your high school classes on a weekly basis
Learn excellent study skills by Dec of junior year
Learn time management by Dec of junior year
Learn techniques for sport you are playing and proper exercise/nutrition by Dec of junior year
Practice SAT and become proficient by end of junior year
Admission essay writing – take a class in writing by end of junior year

Relaxation Training
Complete 10 minutes of relaxation techniques 1x per day for 2 weeks, then as needed to alleviate stress and maintain calm focus

Self-Control Training
Begin exercise program – 3 days a week for 45 minutes/day
Watch no more than 1 hour of television/day on week days, 3 hours on weekends

Internal Locus Training
You believe your English lit teacher doesn't like you and scores your essay exams lower. Concentrate on getting A's on all the multiple choice exams instead. Ask the teacher for guidance.

Support Mechanisms
Ask your most respected teacher to help you through the process as a mentor. Meet with him or her after school once a week for a half hour to review progress.
Tell your family that you are trying to get into an Ivy League school and you'd like their help staying motivated and avoiding distractions.

First Step
Buy an SAT guidebook and study it for 10 minutes every day, starting this Monday

Contingency Plans
Your younger sibling often plays loud music in the evening while you study. You can study in basement, at library, or get some classical music to play that will offset the distraction
Classmates may pick on you for being a nerd or elitist as they find out about your achievements. It will get better when you get to school with people similar to yourself.
Tiredness. It's hard to add extra studying to the already full workload. You know that there are days when you will want to just come home and go straight to bed. Just a few minutes of extra study per day will yield big results.

Goal Journal – Treasure what you Measure

Start a spreadsheet with all your goals and components so you can track them each on a weekly and monthly basis.

Example 2: Army Ranger

Sub Goals
Score high enough on the Army ASVAB to go to Ranger School in 3 months
Get in shape to score 200 on Army Physical Fitness Test in 6 months
Run 5 miles in under 40 minutes in next 2 years
Become qualified as Expert Marksman in 3 years
Learn the Ranger Creed in 1 year

Milestones
Basic Training (6 months)
Advanced Infantry Training (2 years)
Jump School (3 years)
Ranger School (5 years)
Run times for 5 miles: 50 minutes, 48, 46, 44, 42, 40, 38.
Pushups: 40, 50, 55, 60, 65, 70, 75

Year 1 Action Plan
Goals: Complete Basic Training; score 240 on Army Physical Fitness Test; run five miles in 43 minutes; memorize complete Ranger Creed.

Month 1 Action Plan
Goals: Memorize first two sentences of Ranger Creed; complete 45 pushups in two minutes; run five miles in 46 minutes; take ASVAB and get high enough to enter Ranger School.

Week 1 Action Plan
Goals: Meet recruiter; take ASVAB practice test; begin daily workouts; read Ranger Creed 3 times.

Tasks

Practice ASVAB
Do push-ups
Do sit-ups
Run
Go to rifle range
Memorize Ranger Creed

Knowledge
Learn about the ASVAB test and how it's scored
Learn about Army Ranger history and traditions
Read military magazines, watch military movies and T.V. documentaries
Read military biographies
Learn proper foot care
Learn running technique
Read about military tactics, leadership
Read up on Army rules/regulations, the pipeline to Ranger School, military jargon

Skills/Components
Practice land navigation/orienteering
Participate in 3k and 5k races, practice distance running
Hiking and outdoor camping/survival
Shooting skills

Relaxation Training
Complete 10 minutes of relaxation techniques 1x per day for 2 weeks, then as needed to alleviate stress and maintain calm focus

Self-Control Training
Develop 6 day a week exercise program geared towards muscular and cardiovascular endurance to pass the Army and Ranger tests
Practice remaining calm and silent when talked down to at work
2 times a week sleep in a sleeping back with your clothes on

Internal Locus Training
Don't listen to anyone who dismays your goal or says you can't make it. Your friends may laugh at your loss of muscle mass as you go for endurance, laugh with them. Be humble about it. Not everyone will understand your desire.

Support Mechanisms
Ask the Army recruiter if there is anyone in the area who has passed Ranger school that could be your mentor
Try to find someone with similar endurance goals to be your workout partner. Set some targets together and help one another out

First Step
Contact an Army recruiter next Wednesday and schedule a date to take the ASVAB

Contingency Plans
You know that until you head to Basic Training you will have to keep working and fit your preparation around your schedule. Sometimes they make you work extra hours so this will affect the consistency of your efforts.
There is always the possibility you are injured during Army training and your pathway might be delayed.
You know that you will have to deal with extreme exhaustion and sleep-deprivation during the Ranger School. You will have to be ready to function well without full rest.

Goal Journal - Treasure what you Measure
Get a notepad and write down the exercise plan and weekly goals for push-ups, sit-ups and run times. Jot down the other components of the Action Plan. Keep it updated from each workout and review it weekly for other components

Example 3: Business Owner

Sub Goals
Get a cosmetology degree within 3 years

Work part time in a salon for 2 years of the next 5 years
Take basic classes in accounting, finance and marketing within 3 years
Find a location for your business within 4 years
Pay off your current debt within 5 years

Milestones
Get a Cosmetology degree (3 years)
Work in a salon (5 years)
Learn how a salon runs (7 years)
Write a business plan (8 years)
Secure funding (9 years)
Build Out Space (10 years)
Hire Staff (10 years)
Open Salon (10 years)

Year 1 Action Plan
Goals: Hit budget goals; get accepted to school and begin classes; visit 2 top salons/month; take one class in business components.

Month 1 Action Plan
Goals: Ask ten people about their salon likes; go to one trade show; visit mall two times; find a mentor and approach; find possible cosmetology schools and begin applications.

Week 1 Action Plan
Goals: Read industry magazine; begin exercise program and self-control training; tell family of your plan; build budget to pay off debt.

Tasks
Study cosmetology chapters
Cut hair in salon
Write business plan pages
Sign-up for classes
Search for business location
Save money to pay off debt

Knowledge
Subscribe to fashion magazines and small business magazines
Watch style oriented TV programs
Visit malls regularly to see what new fashions are coming out
Go to salon shows and trade conventions
Visit some top-notch salons
Start asking people what they like/dislike about salons and forming your own value proposition – what will set your salon apart
Read biographies of successful entrepreneurs
Attend some chamber of commerce and other business development groups

Skills/Components
Learn how to cut hair, do nails etc.
Financial analysis
Marketing
People management
Customer service training
Networking

Relaxation Training
Complete 10 minutes of breathing techniques 1x per day for 2 weeks, then as needed to alleviate stress and maintain calm focus

Self-Control Training
Start exercise routine – 45 minute spinning class 3x per week
Budget restrictions – set amounts for how much you will spend on pleasure items every month, use the extra money to pay off debt and save

Internal Locus Training
Your company awards bonuses for how the local division does. Don't worry about how the whole division does. Instead concentrate on hitting goals for your branch and try

to raise the level of work for your co-workers at that branch. Make your branch the best in the division.

Support Mechanisms
Find someone locally who has been successful at business and see if the person will be your mentor through the process. It could even be your boss at your present position.
Tell your kids of your desired goal and your reasons for it. Ask them to help you see it to fruition and make it a family effort.
If you know anyone else that wants to get into the industry, become battle buddies and go through the cosmetology schooling and such together.

First Step
Starting Sunday, read 1 industry related magazine a week for the next 3 weeks

Contingency Plans
You know getting a loan from a bank for a start-up is difficult. You may have to get part of the funding from friends and family. Either avenue will be very critical and picky about your business plan. You will need to avoid taking it personally.
Your kids might not want what you want. That's okay, You will do your thing and let them see it and decide for themselves.
A lot of what you need to learn to be successful will be very boring. Be prepared for some dry moments along the way.

Goal Journal - Treasure what you Measure
Make a separate chart of goals, subgoals and components for each of the next 5 years. Break it down into months. Track your progress and update every Sunday evening as you plan and renew commitment for that week's activities.

Step 4: Adapt and Conquer

Part A: Mind over Matter

> "Do your worst, and we will do our best."
> -Winston Churchill

The planning stages are now completed. The blueprint is finalized. We have defined our specific building blocks of success. We know the pitfalls to expect and have means to mitigate their ability to delay us. We are ready. We can begin putting our plans to action.

A thorough vision increases mental toughness and expedites achievement. But the unexpected is inevitable. We will have to adjust on the fly. It's a given, nothing ever works exactly as planned. We will become masters at adaptation and revision. We will become unflappable – invincible – to the vagaries of life.

Just as important will be dealing with what is certain - fatigue, pain, lulls in confidence, sacrifice, disappointment, hardship, struggle - temptation to quit. Nothing great can ever be done without paying a price in sweat. That we will prevail is certain, but in the fog of war it is easy to let that vision wane. But only if we allow it. And we won't.

We will now deal with the execution of our intentions. We will develop iron determination and unbreakable resolve. Our mental toughness and will power will become like granite. And these are the concepts and techniques that will do it.

Awareness

The human mind is an astounding thing. It is our greatest asset. Our ability to reason is what sets us at the top of the food chain. But left unchecked, it can also be our greatest enemy.

The majority of losses are actually losses to ourselves. Our opponents don't beat us; life doesn't beat us; we lose first to our own minds. In fact, in the end, your own mind is the one and only thing that can beat you. But we won't let it.

To keep yourself in the right frame of mind you want to begin cultivating Awareness. You need to be conscious at all times of what is going in and out of your mind. It is a door that must be guarded closely. You need to know what is occupying that space – who is in that room?

Don't let unconscious emotions play tricks on you. Identify them like weeds and pull them out. As soon as you feel negative emotions gnawing at you, pulling you down, splintering your thoughts – identify them. Search yourself. Where is this anxiety coming from? Why do I feel dread? What is it I am afraid of? What is the source of this weight I feel pulling me down?

Once we identify the source of our negative thoughts/feelings we are able to counter-act them with reason. The sooner we find the root of our anxieties the less damage they can do. This process is how we win the Emotional Tug of War.

> Emotional Tug of War: the constant battle to maintain a healthy, productive mental state; controlling our thoughts and emotions to maintain positive vs. negative, optimism vs. pessimism, belief vs. doubt

The human emotional response network is a great warning system, but it has a strong tendency to err on the side of caution. It holds us back. It serves to protect us. But it can also rob us of efficiency and limit our accomplishments. Therefore we must monitor it.

We accomplish this by increasing our self awareness and abilities of introspection through simple practice. The hustle-bustle of modern life does not lend itself to meditation, so we must make the time.

A simple 10 minutes of uninterrupted quiet reflection will do wonders to keep us focused and aware of our emotional state. Create a slot in your schedule for this. In the morning before you leave, on your lunch break, right before bed, or any consistent time you can find.

Locate a calm space, push the immediate concerns of the day to the back of your mind, and meditate. Discover what forces are at play behind your immediate consciousness. Let your emotions bubble to the surface and identify their sources. Reason with yourself to realign your Focused Energy towards your goals. Re-commit to your undertakings. Utilize your V-Day images to direct your emotions.

Doubt is a tumor that we must remove early. It is the precursor to quitting. "I can't" comes right before "I won't." Push out all self-doubts and pessimism. And always take pleasure in where you are in your journey. Let it be a subjective experience that fits your personality, but with the goal of clearing your mind of distractions, calming and renewing your focus on the goals towards which you strive.

> *Pick a time and place to begin making quiet reflection a part of your daily schedule. Begin practicing self awareness as soon as possible.*

The more you practice Awareness the better you will become at the Emotional Tug of War. This is a key to mental toughness. A consciousness of your inner emotions will become like second nature. You will eventually be able to immediately sense negativity seeping into your mind and quash it before it impacts your momentum.

The Warning System

As organisms we strive to remain in a state of homeostasis. We act to maintain equilibrium. It is a natural survival instinct. In the wild, animals generally only leave the safety of their nest, cave or other place of refuge to find food or to reproduce. Humans usually have some loftier goals, which have the unpleasant side effect of taking us well outside our comfort zone. As we sense these alterations and bump into these accustomed barriers we activate the Warning System.

> Warning System – the body/mind reaction to stresses as we approach our habitual limits; our self-preservation alarm; the automatic response to perceived threats; the primary source of suggestions to slow down or give up

This is similar to the dashboard of a jet fighter. There are clusters of instruments and gauges – or in our case sensations and thoughts – that are correlated in varying degrees to specific dangers. They keep us informed of present conditions and immediately alert us whenever a change or new risk factor is detected.

The Sympathetic and Parasympathetic Systems are the main physiological components of this phenomenon. Commonly referred to as "fight or flight", these are the largely involuntary changes our body undergoes to prepare us for action: a stressor triggers response from the hypothalamus deep in the brain through the sympathetic branch of the automatic nervous system to stimulate the adrenal medulla. Fight or flight nervousness ensues, with release of adrenaline. Simultaneously, from the pituitary gland and adrenal cortex comes cortisol, the stress hormone that depletes the brain of neurotransmitters, effecting mood and motivation. The heart rate increases, blood is pulled from the extremities to the vital organs, our senses sharpen, our awareness is heightened and our vision narrows.

This is what we would think of as a "code red", the most aggressive physiological response in our arsenal. This is our onboard computer telling us to "take evasive maneuvers".

The effects of this biological shield are very powerful. In the correct circumstances they are vital to our survival. But when they are clicked on at the wrong time, such as in a debate with one's spouse or while trying to steady one's hand to quickly unlock a door, they can be detrimental to our desired ends.

When the perceived threat is less drastic and urgent in nature, our Warning System is likewise less severe in its response. As a swimmer does a few laps and gets into a workout, the shoulder and back muscles slowly begin to ache and burn. The body is telling us that we are running low on energy reserves and waste byproduct is accumulating in the muscles.

This is a slow, methodical, cautionary feedback system – like the airplane gauges reading low fuel. The onboard computer is bringing something to our attention but not demanding immediate action.

Distorted Perceptions

Researchers Proffitt, Bhalla, Gossweiler and Midgett have done some extraordinary experiments in the field of psychology called Embodied Perception. They found that when having an athlete estimate the slant of a hill, an athlete guesses that the hill is significantly steeper (nearly 10%) when fatigued. Same hill, same athlete, but the perception when exhausted is altered. Our perceptions become distorted under duress.

Similar experiments found that people wearing heavy backpacks or having back pain estimate distances to be greater than they actually are. Point: when tasks become difficult, sensory input is exaggerated to caution us that it will take extra effort. These are *distorted perceptions*. Same hill, same athlete, but in a fatigued state it will take extra effort. The intuition may be correct, but that is a decision we want to make with our mental control center - not our bodies and not our emotions. We want to remain in control. That is mental toughness.

Second Wind

A conscientious person might think, "The Warning System is obviously in place to protect us, so maybe it is not such a great idea to attempt to mitigate it." The problem is, the Warning System is not authentic to our true limitations, but rather our accustomed limitations. It is partly a product of habit, which we will discuss shortly. Secondly, it errs on the side of caution. Like the low gas level indicator on your car, it goes off when there is still something left in the tank. In our case, the tank is often still half full, or more.

Have you ever gone on a long road trip, say 8 hours, and had serious discomfort at the 4 or 5 hour mark, then by the time you got to 7 or 8 hours you feel fine and decide to go on another 2-3 hours? Or during a long day in the office, you feel like you just crashed completely at 10AM, and then by the time 5:30 rolls around you are feeling fine and put in some extra time to get a jump-start on the next day?

What we are talking about here is getting your Second Wind. In essence what happens is you have ignored your Warning System for so long, it gives up and your body goes into over-drive to get the job done. Your body tried to take control early, you didn't let it, and now it lets you be the boss again. Extreme athletes often experience this. They go through a period of muscle fatigue and discomfort, break through the pain barrier, and then enter a period of relative numbness. Often times this is the result of your brain releasing Dopamine and Endorphins, powerful neurotransmitters that increase feelings of wellness and motivation while acting as painkillers. So to some extent you do literally become numb.

It is said that during Navy SEALs initial training period, (during which candidates go through physical training for 5 straight days with only a few hours of sleep, while jumping in and out of frigid water and doing thousands of torturous push-ups, sit-ups etc.) the soldier breaks down to what he thinks is his physical limit of exhaustion, and then, if he is mentally strong enough to stick around, he experiences a Second Wind in which he actually becomes stronger and feels less pain – the body adapts and the last day is easier than the first, despite being in a state of near delirium from lack of sleep and lactic acid buildup. This teaches the future SEALs that they can push way past their perceived limitations, and solidifies the mental toughness they are famous for.

The point you have to always remember is that the pain, fatigue, and stress can not last forever. You can break through it, and your body will adapt. Your ability to adapt is amazing, and you need to have confidence in it. Know your body's reactions and know how to assuage them, and you will accomplish more, much more, than you thought possible.

> *Write down a barrier you want to break through. It can be in exercise, work tasks, habit forming or anywhere you feel like you hit a wall. Incrementally increase effort until you feel yourself get a Second Wind and lunge forward. Realize how much you can do beyond what your Warning System tells you.*

Habits

"We cannot become what we need to be by remaining what we are."
-Max DuPree

It's important to note that the Warning System is not only activated during times of intense exertion. We humans are creatures of habit. Whenever we break a routine we will go through similar reactions to a perceived threat.

Changes to diet, sleeping patterns, social interaction and activity are all capable of triggering similar physiological alert mechanisms. It has been found that people going through break-ups have very similar brain activation to someone in rehab for drug abuse – both sets of people are in effect going through withdrawal. Hearing the voice of your "ex" will actually release chemicals that make you feel better in the short term. Habits are strong and must therefore be watched carefully.

Your body, including your brain, gets used to certain chemicals and stimulations – or lack thereof – and initially rebels against the changes we undertake. We are also re-writing the brain's memory structures, which develop pathways similar to the way the family dog wears a path across the yard towards its favorite shade tree.

The brain has what is called "plasticity", which means it is constantly changing and adapting to the way it is used. "Use it or lose it." You are actually changing the physical structure of your brain by your actions. This gives you a powerful ability to improve yourself. Research has found that athletes develop thicker and thicker outer layers to their brains (governing learning and movement) the longer they play a sport, and professional athletes emit stronger alpha waves than normal, which shows they are able to act more on instinct and many of their activities have become automatic.

Your brain is largely what you make it. It is very adaptable. Practice math, and your brain restructures itself to perform math. Sing every day, and your brain becomes better at music. Perform mental toughness training and over time your brain will grow and adapt to have greater and greater discipline. Through your choices and actions you are in a constant state of becoming what you are. Your brain reacts to the stimulus you place on it just as muscles respond to exercise, and similarly this specific adaptation carries with it some amount of discomfort.

Expect a "withdrawal" period as you break old habits and form new ones. This has been found to typically last for less than 30 days.

Note: You can think of your overall personality like concrete – it stiffens with age. Up till about age 30 our traits and preferences are relatively soft and pliable, and by our 50's we are becoming fairly rigid. You always have the ability to change, but keep in mind as you age the process will take a bit longer.

> *Write down the date which you have begun to alter a certain habit or routine. Count down 30 days and realize that you have the power to make yourself whatever you want to be.*

Emotional Warning System - Stress

> "The only thing we have to fear is fear itself."
> -FDR

There is, as with everything humans do, an intellectual and emotional element of the Warning System as well. If our physical warning cues are pain and fatigue, our mental warning cues are anxiety and tension.

Anger is the pinnacle of emotional preservation. Anger is used to alleviate perceptions of severe emotional threat. It is a dire action of defense, akin to "circling the wagons" or a Blowfish puffing out its spiky spines. If you pay attention, you will note that there is always an undertone of panic in an angry person. In our fighter plane, this is equivalent to shooting off all your guns and missiles at once in an act of desperation.

The more common emotion used by the Warning System is stress - like the gnawing sensation you get being around your arrogant, condescending boss, or the unease and apprehension that keeps you up at night when you have to give an important speech the next day. What it is telling you is that there is a threat to your equilibrium, that you are unsafe, and that you should alter your course. But sometimes there is no alternative course.

So the Warning System is in place to preserve and conserve, to protect and defend. It lets us know when there is some danger to us - either physical or mental - through our sensations of pain, fatigue, fear and anxiety. It is a useful tool and vital to our self-preservation, but it also has a tendency to place limitation on us and prevent us from making gains towards our goals. It sets limits on our abilities and makes a fuss when we desire to move those limits. It tells us to slow down, and it often wants us to quit altogether.

As was mentioned briefly, much of what we overcome in our Emotional Tug of War comes directly from the Warning System. It is the origin of much negative thought. You are struggling to complete a presentation or finish a midterm paper and something inside is telling you, "You can't do this. You are too tired. It's too difficult." That is the voice of your Warning System.

Because the Warning System is designed to conserve, it often acts irrationally. It almost universally stops us before it needs to. Imagine if we gave up every time we felt tension or discomfort – we would never accomplish anything. Remember, we can do more than we think we can, much more. Often 3 or 5 times more - but only when we can overcome the suggestions of our Warning System.

Remember, this is a tug of war. Either your body is going to tell you what it *wants* to do or you are going to tell your body what it *will* do. At some point the body will win. Everyone has physical limits. But you have no idea what those limits really are until you take control and start moving them. The techniques in this chapter will give you that control – they allow you to delay the Warning System and force your body to adjust to higher and higher levels of output.

You have massive, MASSIVE reserves!

When you obey the Warning System you are the slave, and you have limitations. These methods will make you the master, and you will have the power to move those limitations.

Case Study: There was an experiment done in which competitive weight lifters were asked to perform a one-rep maximum bench press. The participants were then hypnotized and told they could lift more than their previous best lift. The hypnotist walked them through a visualization of completing the exercise at the higher weight. The participants then tried a second one-rep maximum with overwhelming success. This illustrates the power of belief in your ability and that your body naturally holds you below your true potential.

Once we cultivate our awareness and are able to recognize the work of the Warning System, we can begin to supervise it, delay it and over-ride when need be. Mental toughness means we decide when there is something really wrong that we need to address, and when we are just receiving a warning that needs to be controlled, not obeyed. We will discuss specific techniques for this in Part B.

Begin noticing and identifying your Warning System in action. Write down a few examples of times your Warning System was initiated over the last week. Did you obey it? Did you need to?

Fluid Adaptation

"We will either find a way or make one."
-Hannibal

One of the Warning System's most potent trigger mechanisms is Change. When we are in the thick of pursing our goals and making steady progress, it's almost certain something will spring up that we must react to - the proverbial curve ball.

Few things will activate that alarm system like the unexpected. This is why moving is cited as the most stressful common life occurrence after bereavement and divorce - it's the uncertainty and feeling of powerlessness. It's that element of unknown that accompanies change - that lack of control, sense of helplessness, loss of future vision, insecurity, ambiguity, vagueness - it causes fear. We don't know what to expect. It makes us want to retreat. It fosters doubt. And we don't like doubt. Doubt is our mortal enemy.

The ability to handle change can make or break a goal, and it usually does. Overcoming an unexpected hurdle becomes your tipping point towards invincible mental toughness.

When the going gets tough, the tough... adapt.

Once we let that fear and doubt stifle us we lose all Focused Energy. Our momentum grinds to a halt. We are going along, hitting Sub-Goals and Milestones, making progress, growing belief and confidence, when we hit a snag. Something unexpected happens. We are thrown off our base, side-swiped, dismayed. Frustration mounts.

75

During unexpected changes is the easiest time to quit, bar none. But we won't quit. We will revise, alter, adjust or innovate, but we won't quit. Quitting isn't even a word we let enter into our minds. We will follow the model of a successful organism.

Successful Organism:

Change in Environment + Adaptation = Survival

Unsuccessful Organism:

Change in Environment + No Adaptation = Extinction

This is fairly self-explanatory. Substitute "progress" or "accomplishment" for *Survival* and "no progress" or "failure" for *Extinction* and this fits our model. To drive this point home we will develop the idea into a cause and effect equation.

Here are our premises:

1) Homeostasis is an organisms attempt to remain in its current condition. Newton observed that "Objects at rest stay at rest." Therefore, resistance to change is normal. We naturally lament the loss of our equilibrium, our accustomed state.
2) The body is a Warning System. Its job is to preserve. It wants you to quit, to hold back, to maintain a safety buffer. You can do much more than you think.
3) Limitations are largely imposed by your habits, by friends, family or by society. We have the ability to reset the Warning System.
4) Stress, pain, fatigue and doubt are all part of the Warning System. They are largely subjective. We waste critical energy attempting to maintain homeostasis.

5) Accepting new conditions creates a new homeostasis. Accepting the altered state disarms your body's alarms.

From these premises we deduce the Law of Constant Homeostasis.

Law of Constant Homeostasis: you are only out of equilibrium until you accept the new conditions; recognizing the fresh paradigm resets limitations and lowers perceived stress

As soon as we accept new conditions we have returned ourselves to a new state of equilibrium. The vacuum closes. A new homeostasis emerges. And our progress can continue. This doesn't mean we return to the previous state, but that the new state becomes your expectation. If your leg is broken, your leg is broken. But once you accept that as a fact and stop fighting it, your critical warning system can be taken off of alert (or at least reduced) and you can return to the objectives at hand.

"Don't sweat it, reset it."

This is simply saying that we can't make progress until we cease rejecting our situation. We must embrace conditions we can't change. We must adapt. "Don't curse the dark, turn on the lights." But as humans we do spend a lot of time cursing the dark – complaining, moping, regretting, thinking of what-ifs, if-onlys and what-could-have-beens – plain old bellyaching.

In psychology jargon we want to "decrease emotionally-focused coping" and "increase problem-focused coping" – stop lamenting and start resolving.

"Are we going to sit around moaning or are we going to do something about it?" Call it self pity, call it feeling sorry for yourself or call it our inbred desire to maintain homeostasis, it is a cancer to accomplishment. High achieving people don't lament, they adapt. They don't see obstacles, they see challenges - challenges that will make the victory even sweeter. And they don't waste time brooding over what's thrown at them, they simply react and move on.

This requires emotional control, objective-focus and contingency planning. All of which we have already started to cultivate.

To function well in an environment that is constantly changing and often out of our control we must be able to respond with Fluid Adaptation.

> **Equation of Fluid Adaptation:** The longer it takes a subject to recognize, accept and adapt to new conditions, the less efficient our energy expenditure is, the less progress we make and the longer and harder success becomes

This is to say that there is an inverse relationship between time to acceptance and progress made. The more time it takes to accept and adapt, the less progress is made; the less time it takes to accept and adapt, the more progress is made.

The faster you adapt, the more momentum you keep and the more progress you make.

Time to Accept → = Progress ←

Time to Accept ← = Progress →

"You snooze, you lose." Here's an example. There are few work environments with the psychological challenges and anxiety that Wall Street poses. Every day is a constant struggle between optimism and pessimism ("bulls and bears"), greed and fear, on a global scale. Those who are successful have to be masters of mental/emotional discipline and have an uncanny ability to adapt at a moment's notice.

The axiom stock traders use is "the market is always right". You may pick a stock that posts huge numbers and handily beats expectations on the day of reported earnings. And its price may fall anyway. You have two choices: hang on and hope, or cut your losses and move on. As you sit and wonder "why?", as you stare in disbelief and shake your fists, it continues to plummet.

"Denial is futile." The longer you stay in denial, the more money you are losing. The market has spoken. Move on. The faster you do so, the sooner you can get start making money again. What "should be" does not matter, only what is. This is not an easy thing to do, and that's why the traders who can do it are rewarded so handsomely. They are masters of Fluid Adaptation.

> **Fluid Adaptation**: the ability to quickly accept changes in conditions, react to new information and adjust seamlessly to minimize loss of momentum; capacity to maintain sense of homeostasis in unstable environment

We see in this example the same inverse relationship – the longer it takes the trader to accept and react with a new plan, the less progress (and in this case profit) is made. The time spent metaphorically "cursing the dark" is pure opportunity cost.

> "These are the times that try men's souls."
> -Thomas Paine

Responding to uncertainty is what sets apart the great from the good. We all know the feeling of "having the rug pulled out from under you" – those evil, unforeseen twists and changes that take our breath away. Our reaction of shock and dismay is normal and healthy, but these are emotions we must be able to regulate and train.

If we let our emotions control us our energy becomes divided and our efficiency plummets. We are scattered. We miss opportunities and we begin to digress if not outright give up. We are stifled.

This is why we spent time working on contingency planning for distractions. Since we have already mentally prepared we can keep our time to accept and adapt to a minimum. Think of change as distraction on an epic scale.

> *Build on your Contingency Planning. Add potential changes, new conditions and effective adaptations. Build in a couple worst-case scenarios.*

"Expect the unexpected." Prepare for the worst and you will do your best. If this is done thoroughly, nothing will be able to knock you off your base. Our progress may be slowed at times, but it will never be halted.

> "No plan survives contact with the enemy."
> -Helmuth von Moltke

There is one, and only one, question we care about: "What is the best, fastest way to deal with this problem?" What do I need to *do*? What is my *next* step? Every other thought and emotion is inefficiency.

The analogy for what we want to exhibit is water. Imagine a stream rolling down the hill. The water molecules do not worry about the obstacles they meet. These happy little molecules abide by the simple principle of following the shortest path to their destination. If you put a rock in a stream, the water simply goes around it, again in the shortest path possible. They follow the path of least resistance. They practice fluid adaptation, literally. We will strive to become like water, always moving with singular purpose towards our destination, moving over or around any obstacle in our path.

Quick, effective reaction to change is the offspring of mental toughness. This is how elite athletes, entrepreneurs and leaders of all kinds react to new challenges. Adaptation is essential to achievement.

> "Change is the law of life."
> -John F. Kennedy

Examples

Example 1: Ivy League University

Awareness Training
While waiting for the morning bus, spend 10 minutes in reflection per day. Identify emotions, concerns and sources of stress. Can be combined with relaxation techniques.

Second Wind
You feel exhaustion after studying for 45 minutes. Use one page Micro Goals to break through to the two hour studying mark. Your mind starts to refocus at about the one hour and twenty minute mark.

Habits
Begin a habit of looking up in the dictionary every word you don't know. Count 30 days.

Warning System
Activated due to fatigue while studying, while exercising, when given a long essay to write.

Fluid Adaptation

You can't get the SAT score your top school wants. Bolster your extracurricular activities instead.

You don't get in to the school you want or can't afford it. You go to a junior college for a year and reapply.

Example 2: Army Ranger

Awareness Training
During your lunch break, spend 10 minutes in reflection per day. Identify emotions, concerns and sources of stress. Can be combined with relaxation techniques.

Second Wind
You get stuck at 40 push-ups. Rest 30 seconds in push-up position then do another 10 push-ups. Lower the rest period and raise the second push-up number until you can do 60 push-ups. Track your Percentage to Completion.

Habits
Begin shaving every morning. Count 30 days.

Warning System
Activated while running, doing push-ups, long roadmarch. Activated while drill instructor was yelling at platoon.

Fluid Adaptation
Your ASVAB score is too low to become a Ranger. You study for the test and retake it.

You get an injury during Ranger School. You adjust to it and continue on, or if debilitated you come back to try again as soon as possible.

During training your platoon gets in trouble and is punished. Use it as a chance to show leadership and uplift your comrades.

During a land navigation it begins to pour rain. It will be cold and slippery. Slow down, close up as much as possible, and continue on coordinates carefully.

Example 3: Business Owner

Awareness Training
Before bed, spend 10 minutes in reflection per day. Identify emotions, concerns and sources of stress. Can be combined with relaxation techniques.

Second Wind
You get too bored to study your accounting text more than 15 minutes. Play some music beforehand and visualize V-Day, then decide to Do It Anyway and add five minutes until you can study for 45 minutes.

Habits
Never leave your house without make-up on and your hair done. Count 30 days.

Warning System
Activated during exercise, while filling out applications for school, while telling family of plans, during traffic jam.

Fluid Adaptation
Styles of hair are constantly adapting. Stay on top of the trends
You can't get a loan. You will have to continue working, try to manage a salon and look for someone who could be a business partner.

Part B: In the Heat of Battle

"Pressure makes diamonds."
-Gen George Patton

We will now discuss the specific methods used to win the daily internal and external battles. Think of it as your arsenal or toolbox. It's a skill-set. You may not use all the techniques, and you will definitely use some more than others. The more tools you have at your disposal, the greater the chance you will find the one you need when you need it.

Learn them, try them out, practice them, and incorporate them into your own unique, dynamic formula of mental toughness. Some will strike an immediate cord; some work well for particular goals; some you can rotate in and out; some you will keep as back up. Just like a baseball pitcher tries to master as many pitches as possible but always has a few favorites, continue to build your arsenal and increase your repertoire while keeping your priority on doing whatever is most effective for you individually, in your personal path to achievement.

Each recipe of success is slightly different – use what's effective.

F.A.C.E.

"Delta make their own luck." –Delta Force Motto

The first technique we will discuss is the acronym F.A.C.E. and is used to break barriers and adapt to unexpected obstacles. This is a simple, powerful weapon for mastering the Warning System, speeding adaptation and exhibiting mental/emotional control.

1. Face Facts

The process starts with a realization that the situation has changed. This may be obvious, in the case of a physical injury or event recognizable to the senses. If a lightning storm, flat tire or artillery barrage is what we are up against, it won't take trained powers of deduction to detect it.

But in more subtle endeavors, such as the shifting strategy of an opposing tennis player, evolving consumer preferences or the slow diminishment of our health, an alteration in conditions may not be as self-evident. We need to frequently analyze the environments under which we strive, asking ourselves, "Has any significant modification taken place?", "Are we still playing by the same rules?"

Don't practice avoidance of the uncomfortable. Don't live in denial. Don't be the ostrich with your head in the sand. This is the surest way to be left behind. Use your awareness and reflection. Recognize that something is different and it must be dealt with. Attack the problem head on.

Describe objectively the kind and scope of the alteration to circumstances. Make a detailed report of the situation.

2. Accept Situation

As previously discussed, this is the element that involves the most emotions, and is therefore the part where the most difficulty lies. Mankind has a tenacious ability to continue acting on expired information with complete disregard for effectiveness or efficiency. It's like driving a car down the freeway while staring in the rear view mirror. But while mule-like stubbornness may win you a few battles with your spouse, it won't do you any good as you chase your dreams.

We get used to the way things are, we get in a rhythm, we wear in a nice little groove and we react vehemently against anything that disturbs that balance. Normal is comfortable.

Normal is known. We understand the rules and we know what to expect. Normal is predictable. Normal is low stress. There is no impetus to change.

But the world changes and we can't stop it. That "normal" that we knew is gone forever, and holding onto it is simply an exercise in wasteful futility.

"It is what it is." This is a modern phrase that addresses this emotional bind – although the words are nothing more than reflexive, circular logic, its use and meaning states, "we can't change it, we might as well accept it and do the best we can." Said another way, "You can't fight the tide."

Remember, there is one, and only one, question we care about: "What is the best, fastest way to deal with this problem?"

Simply put, when confronted with change we must regain our sense of homeostasis and turn off our critical warning alarms as quickly as possible. We must put all focus on solving the dilemma. To do this, we must first accept the situation. Stop resisting the inevitable, don't try to deny the new circumstances - embrace the challenge. There are two go-to actions for doing this:

Strategy: The New Normal

> "Reject your sense of injury and the injury itself disappears."
> -Marcus Aurelius

One mindset to do this is the "new normal". Once we have identified precisely what is different, we simply think of this as the "new normal." Like setting a watch for a new time zone or aligning the steering in your car, we recalibrate our mind to the fresh set of rules or conditions.

The underpinnings of this have been discussed. As we encounter change or distress, the body's critical warning signals set in and we resist. Whenever we need to break through those barriers or get beyond those new obstacles we must first reset the system. First we assure our body and our mind we must accept and adapt to the current situation – we tell ourselves, "this is the new normal" – then we can get our Warning System calmed down and continue our forward progress.

Suppose you are starting a brutal cardio kickboxing class. Fifteen minutes in you are riddled with pain and want to quit. Your body is telling you something is wrong and you better cease activity. You have activated the Warning System in a big way.

Instead of quitting, you repeat to yourself, "this is the new normal, for the next 45 minutes there will be pain." You have now reset your system and told it to expect some painful muscle fatigue. This won't necessarily make it hurt any less, but it will make the pain less distracting. You basically make the burning sensation a background noise, a soundtrack that you don't concentrate on.

Case Study: Runner Steve Prefontaine was America's premier distance runner in the 1970's. In, Without Limits, a film made about his life, he accounts for his uncanny ability to wear out his opponents, "I can endure more pain than anyone you've ever met. That's why I can beat anyone I've ever met." Of course he also had immense physical gifts, but he counted his biggest advantage as his ability to dissuade his Warning System and push through pain barriers.

Case Study: Eric Haney, in his book "Inside Delta Force", chronicles his experience passing the testing phase for entry into America's most elite military unit. During one stage of the grueling selection process, the candidates are taken to a remote location in the Northeast and tasked with hiking back and forth over a craggy mountain-top in a route that forms a six-pointed star, alone, while wearing a heavy rucksack. The "Day of the Star" is the breaking point for many extremely rugged soldiers - soldiers who have already proven to be of the highest caliber.

Checkpoint after checkpoint, being sent back across the sharp peaks on almost exactly the same route they just came from, the physical and mental strain was unbearable. Haney was exhausted by this "masterful torture" and near his wits' end. Then, he writes, "I had a revelation: What difference could it possibly make if I crossed back and forth over this same mountain until doomsday? A mountain was a mountain, time was time, and route selection was route selection. ... The frustration and mental torture I had been suffering were completely of my own making – and completely within my power to disregard. I dropped all thoughts of anything other than making the best possible approach to the next RV, and it was amazing how much mentally and physically stronger I felt."

The course is designed to test the candidates' ability to cope with stress and the unexpected. Beyond the extreme physical endurance is the test of mental toughness – how do the soldiers handle frustration and ambiguity? Can they maintain focus? Can they adapt? Will they let hopelessness and doubt set in? We can see Haney's evolution as he faces the situation for what it is, accepts it as the new normal – the status quo - and moves from an emotional focus (frustration) to a problem focus (finding the next checkpoint). He identifies his Warning System, realizes it is within his power to reset his limitations, and disarms it. His mental resistance is fruitless and distracting. He puts his efforts towards the aspects of his situation he has control over, and stops wasting energy thinking about anything else.

Case Study: George St. Pierre is considered one of the top mixed martial arts fighters of all time. Early in his title defense against Jake Shields, St Pierre suffered an inadvertent eye gouge. The following is the dialogue he had with his coach Greg Jackson in between rounds:

St. Pierre - "I can't see with my left eye."

Jackson - "It doesn't matter. You've got one eye, its fine. Listen to me, George. Ignore that, you've got one eye, you're fine. Look at me. You're fine. You can see me, you can see the punches. Now listen. Relax, calm down, find your center."

St. Pierre's coach, considered one of the best in the business, tells him to accept the loss of the use of his left eye as the new normal. "You've got one eye, you're fine." This is the new situation he must accept. Jackson coaches him to practice emotional control, relaxation and awareness ("find your center"). The injury has activated St. Pierre's Warning System – for good reason – he is far outside his comfort zone. They adjusted the strategy to keep some extra distance and utilized St. Pierre's jab. He won a unanimous decision.

Think about those who were in real estate before the market collapse in the late 2000's. If you were an agent or someone flipping houses the chances are you saw a huge drop in your ability to make money, almost overnight. There are some who still have not accepted the change in circumstances. They are still out there, scraping by and waiting for the market to bounce back. In the meantime, there are other ways to make ends meet. For the vast majority of people in the real estate industry, the correct move was to accept that the housing slump was the "new normal", stop looking backwards and to adapt by re-tooling occupational skills to stay afloat until the sun shines on housing once more.

Identify some situations of change or distress in your life that you should accept as the "new normal".

Reset your expectations. Repeat it to yourself when you feel the Warning System kicking in.

Strategy: Do it Anyway

This is our second technique for accepting changed conditions and alleviating the emotional bind of the Warning System: we admit the negative aspects of the change, but tell ourselves, "Do it anyway."

Imagine you are 3/4ths of the way through a grueling swim race or 12 hour UPS delivery shift and your body just wants to rest. You think to yourself, "Yes, this hurts, it feels awful right now, but I am going to do it anyway." Unlike the previous technique that centers around resetting perceived norms and zeroing the alarms, this technique admits the Warning System has a point, but simply disregards it. Admitting is a big part of accepting and dropping resistance.

You don't want to get out of bed in the morning, but you do it anyway. Your body tells you to stop studying and go to bed, but you finish the studying anyway. Most combat soldiers will admit they get nervous before a battle, but they trust in their training and "soldier on" – they do it anyway. The fear, anxiety, fatigue or whatever else your warning system is throwing at you – you simply ignore it. First you admit the point – "yes, this is dangerous", "yes, I'm exhausted", "yes, I don't know what to expect" – then you throw those concerns behind you and carry on.

When the going gets tough, the tough... do it anyway.

There's an amazing power in admitting someone has a point – it's completely disarming. Try it. Next time your boss or your spouse is going on about something, simply say, "Yes you're right, you have a point." It takes the wind right out of their sails, leaves them speechless. It's strange to think, but this is the same thing we do towards ourselves, with our own interior conversation – stop the debate. End the argument. Send the message to your Warning System, "Yes, I heard you, now pipe down I have work to do."

"Yes lungs, you are right, you're tired."

"Yes, I know, calling back these 10 clients with the updated price quotes is going to be very stressful. I will catch a lot of flak."

"Yes, I'll now have to re-run every experiment. My 4 hour day just went to 11 hours."

"Yes, I know Ranger school has a high drop-out rate. These coming weeks will be no cake walk."

"Yes, it's awful that I tore a ligament in my knee and I can't make the same moves. I can still help my team."

We can listen to the Warning System, hear it out, and then disavow it. Admission will stop the internal dialogue and quiet the Warning System. Now, we can refocus our efforts and continue our progress.

> *Write down a few situations where you have to overcome resistance to change or discomfort in order to make progress. Admit to the difficulty but decide to "do it anyway".*

In time these mental processes will become second nature, automatic. You will be able to intuitively sense a change, accept it, and immediately begin looking for your next step. A good coach, director or general will drop his or her carefully wrought plans in an instant – the very second he or she realizes something has changed. It is fluid and immediate and done without regrets or remorse. And that is because the goal trumps all petty concerns and emotional hang ups.

3. Consider Options

Once we have accepted the new conditions, calmed our body's defense systems and stopped fighting against the inevitable, we are back in the fight. We still have work to do, but the important thing is we are moving in the right direction. We have maintained our Focused Energy.

Every time we encounter a shift in our environment of operation, we should reconsider our options. If the plan we have laid out is still the best one, no problem. If our goals, time-frames and objectives are no longer feasible or have become inefficient, there is a new plan needed.

If we are trying to hit a certain sales number in our business and there is a terrorist attack or something else that causes a huge decrease in demand, we need to adjust our targets and manage expenses. If the government changes industry regulations, we need to alter how we do things and reassess profit margins. If an aspiring singer with his or her heart set on Nashville comes down with laryngitis, it is logical to alter our plans to take this into account. We adjust on the fly, reacting with a change in goals or strategies as we see fit, and continue on.

We deal with instability by re-accessing the path of least resistance. We determine our options in light of the new circumstances. If we are still on the straightest path we simply continue, and if a new plan is needed we adjust accordingly.

Write down several alternative strategies you could employ to realize your goals. Weigh the benefits and costs and decide if alteration is advisable.

4. Execute

If we have done our homework, this step is straightforward. We have maintained our motivation, belief, vision and still have Focused Energy. We revised our plan to fit the new environment. Now we simply take the First Step in the new direction, and continue hitting Milestones towards our Mega Goals.

> *Write down your revised First Step. Put rubber to road.*

Constantly evaluating, accepting and adapting to new circumstances is the only way to thrive in an environment of flux. Mastering this ability takes the factor of chance out of our endeavors and keeps the element of control firmly within our grasp. In moving from passive receptors to active agents we become masters of our destiny.

"So what do we do? Anything. Something. So long as we just don't sit there. If we screw up, start over. Try something else. If we wait until we've satisfied all the uncertainties, it may be too late."
-Lee Iacocca, Former CEO of Chrysler

Micro Visualization

This is your chance to experience success before you begin. Think of it as a full dress rehearsal, a free practice run. Visualization prior to standardized exams been shown to increase scores. We will use the same process of visualization as with Mega Goals and apply it to the immediate challenge at hand.

You will be successful. How are you going to do it? Walk through it in your mind - watch yourself perform - use all your senses and emotions. Feel yourself doing everything right. If you are sitting in the locker room before a football game, go through the specific plays you will perform and moves you will make. If you have to call a client, plan the words you will say, what the client might say, and how you will respond. Concentrate on the tone of voice you will have and how you will approach each objective. Before a mountain bike race, imagine yourself navigating difficult obstacles, the burn you will have in your legs, how you will mentally combat the Tug of War as your body tries to conserve – see yourself taking drinks from your camelback and speeding across the finish line.

Use this technique before difficult workouts to imagine yourself exercising with high energy and stamina. Use it before presentations or dates to decrease anxiety of the unknown. Whatever your immediate challenge is, take a few minutes before you begin to meditate, focus and perform a visual walk-through of your achievement. This is a powerful performance enhancer and confidence booster.

> *Choose a difficult short-term task you must perform. Visually walk through your actions. Think about exactly what you will do and how you will react to your Warning System. Use all your senses as you imagine every aspect of your successful performance.*

Micro goals

For a short recap, we have Mega Goals – the life aspirations that are usually long-term in nature. These constitute the framework of a happy, satisfying, fulfilled life.

We break these down into Sub-Goals and Milestones, which are the skills, studies, components and landmarks that act as gateways to our highest achievements. They set our immediate sights and shape the short-term action plans that we form and implement over weeks, months and years.

And there is an important principle behind this that, once absorbed, becomes an armor that deflects doubt and negativity like water off a duck. This is the principle of Divide and Conquer.

> **Divide and Conquer** – the principle that victory is nothing more than a string of small wins; success is cumulative so the volume of wins matters more than their size; dividing larger goals into smaller and smaller increments as stress increases

Remember: the more difficult conditions become, the smaller and more proximate (immediate) goals need to be. The harder our efforts become, the closer our focus gets. Under duress we must concentrate only on the most immediate task at hand.

So, if our larger goals are feeling overwhelming, we simply chop them into tiny, contiguous successes and start building. As our physical and mental stress mount and our Warning System goes into emergency mode, we have to bring our attention to the immediate task at hand.

We know where we want to be in five years, but how are we going to get through the next ten minutes, the next hour? Narrow your focus to the immediate task at hand. Win by increments.

Running a six minute mile is a tremendous challenge for the average person. But running one lap in 1:30 seconds does not seem so difficult. If we can maintain enough focus to run a 1:30 second lap 4 times in a row, we have run a six minute mile.

Likewise, when a race car driver is in second place with only a few laps to go, he or she does not concentrate on the 10 seconds he has to make up to overtake the leader. Rather the driver concentrates on the very next turn, trying to make it to that turn as quickly as possible, shaving off a second or a half a second at a time. It's the cumulative effect of these tiny efforts that will win the race.

If you were asked, could you do 100 push-ups on the spot? Most people could not. But could you do 10 push-ups? Then take a brief break and do another 10? And another? By the end, as the pain increases, you will end up resting between every push-up. Even if you don't hit the 100 mark, by breaking up the goal into smaller, immediate tasks, you accomplish much, much more than you thought possible.

Remember: You can do much more than your body tells you. Often 3, 5 or 50 times more. You have massive, MASSIVE reserves!

Suppose you have a sales job where you cold-call potential customers every day from 1-5. Thinking about 4 hours of cold-calling is a bear. After 30 or 40 rejections and receiving a few unkind nicknames, you'd rather be anywhere than sitting in that chair, staring at that phone. You look at your list – 200 more names to contact. You get a queasy feeling. It just feels like too much. It feels like it is beyond your limits. But you remember your V-Day image, being the top salesperson and taking your family on that trip to Hawaii – that V-Day image of the Hawaii sunset comes to mind. Alright, let's hunker down. 200 seems insurmountable. But you can do 10, just 10, more calls. You do 10, take a break, praise yourself, and do another 10. And another. 5 good leads. Ten more calls. One particularly obnoxious jerk offends you and really throws you off base. You can feel anxiety creeping up your back muscles. You do a brief relaxation technique. 10 feels like too much. But you can do 5, just 5, more calls. You do 5. You get 2 good leads. Congratulations. You do another 5. And another. You are exhausted. The coffee is wearing off and you are getting hungry. You make 3 calls. 3 more calls. 3 more calls. One additional lead. You have some serious doubts about the product, and wonder if you aren't just too soft for this. It's not time to go home yet. Let's just do one more call. You make a call. You take a break. You make another call. You write a couple notes for tomorrow. You make one more call. The next name sounds friendly, so you make another call. It's a lead. You look at the clock. It's 5 P.M. You take a deep breath, shut down your terminal and gather your things.

As you walk out you look over the just-posted break-downs and are amazed, you made almost 70 calls in the last 2 hours and got close to 10 solid leads. More importantly, you maintained momentum, built a string of success and fostered belief and self confidence. Chances are you will accomplish more tomorrow. And you can sleep soundly this evening, knowing that your mental toughness is going to carry you to triumph.

When the going gets tough, the tough... focus on the immediate task at hand.

Keep breaking the goals down, smaller and smaller – as small and close as you need them to be to continue your string of success. At times this will literally mean simply putting one foot in front of the other. Just make it through today; just make it to lunch; just finish this chapter. These small, immediate goals that maintain our momentum are Micro Goals.

> **Micro Goals** – the smallest next step you can take towards you goal; the closest, most immediate success you can achieve with confidence

Suppose you want to run 10 miles today. You run the first couple with no problem. Then 3 miles in you hit a limit and your Warning System starts to kick in. 7 more miles, more than tripling what you've done, is overwhelming. The monkey mind begins chattering - negative thoughts start to enter. First, you remind yourself that this fatigue and exhaustion is the New Normal, it is expected and will last awhile and that is alright. Next you decide that you will do it anyway. Now you break it down into Micro Goals. You aim for 3 more miles. You got it – success. You strive for 2 miles. You win again. You concentrate on 1 more mile and hit it with good times. Now just four more laps. 1... 2... 3... Get through the next straight... One more straight... And you are done. The harder it became, the shorter you made your goals.

Imagine your Sub-Goal is to get a 1200 SAT score so you can get into a certain university. You buy an SAT study book and plan to read it, then take 2 practice tests, then take the SAT. But you become so busy between school, work and sports that you are drained by the time you get some down time to study for the SAT. Think small. Read just one page before you go to bed. When that becomes too difficult, get a list of vocabulary words. Study 2 words per day, once in the morning, once in the evening.

Bit by bit, day by day, you are making progress. Sometimes its slower progress then other times, but the important thing is to stay engaged and keep your momentum. Then, once your schedule frees up – or whatever else is restricting you – you simply ratchet up the intensity of your efforts. Keep dividing your goals into small enough increments to stay on target and stay in the game – realize that the sun sets but the dawn is always coming, and if you just keep plugging away in whatever amount you can the darkness will eventually turn into radiant light.

Think about the smallest steps you can make towards your goals. Write them down. Be ready to bring your focus closer and closer as progress becomes more difficult.

Percentage to Completion

"Many of life's failures are people who did not realize how
close they were to success when they gave up."
-Thomas Edison

Another powerful way to maintain your momentum, increase positive emotions and disable the Warning System is tracking Percentage to Completion. Instead of *dividing up*, this technique entails *adding up* – tracking what we have accomplished as a percentage of the total to enhance our feeling of accomplishment and boost our knowledge of the finish line.

> **Percentage to Completion** – keeping track of the
> fraction or percentage of the way to completion;
> working towards fractional parts of a goal as
> milestones that increase motivation and belief

Let's say we decide to increase our run distance to 12 miles today. We run the first mile and think, "Alright, $1/12^{th}$ done. Not too bad." Then you run the 2nd mile and note to yourself, "Okay, just repeat that 5 more times. No big deal." After your 3rd mile you say, "There we go, a quarter of the way done. 25% there, no problem." At the 6 mile mark, "Here we go, half way. 50% done. All downhill from here." The 8th mile marks 2/3rds, the 9th mile is 75% complete, then 2 laps left, then 1... Finished.

We are conditioned to think in fractions and percentages. From "Now 10% More in Every Bottle!" to "Half-Off Sales" and all the other advertising we are bombarded with, it's a part of our sub-conscious thinking pattern.

And more than that, watching your progress is a natural high – it's part of the organic confidence-building inherent to the goal attainment process. This is simply measuring success on the micro level. Seeing how much you have done and how far you have come is a powerful motivator. The closer you get to your end the more optimistic you become and the greater effort you are likely to give. When we count and realize we are 90% done we start to savor the success and sprinting the final 10% is an exertion we barely even notice.

Something like distance running is an easy example because it lends itself to obvious division. But this can be applied to any endeavor. We can take a lacrosse season and break it down into fractions based on the number of games and practices remaining. Candidates count down the days left until Election Day.

If you decide to start a business or manufacture a product, map out the process and then break it into phases. An example for a product is: Design Phase; Prototype Phase; Testing Phase; Marketing and Packaging; Manufacture and Distribute. We can now track our Percentage to Completion. If you want more detail, break each phase down into individual sub-tasks. This type of mapping is actually a large part of what Project Managers get paid to do, all day, every day.

Likewise, a typical business start-up sequence is: Research and Business Plan; Funding; Location and Build Out; Admin and Advertising Preparation; Grand Opening. Populate each phase with some of the specific tasks they will entail, and then start marking them off as you finish and you can turn the process into a Percentage of Completion. You can also estimate the number of days each phase will take and keep track of your progress towards overall completion.

Remember our principle – as the days become more difficult, the focus has to become more and more near-term. You will probably need to move from the percentage of the entire project down to the percentage of each particular phase and then down to the percentage of individual tasks, such as what percentage of the marketing plan or first year Profit and Loss Statement you have finished working on. Or during Build Out Phase, "Alright, we have 75% of the computer terminals installed and the carpet is half way finished." Remember, the bigger the task and higher the stress, the smaller you will have to think to keep on point.

Any large goal is simply the completion of a string of smaller goals.

"Rome wasn't built in a day."

When it gets difficult and you feel like you are sinking, accomplish the simplest, most immediate thing you can do to move towards your goal, no matter how small it is. When it is feeling impossible, draw your focus in until you find something that is possible.

> *Write down a few instances when it will be motivating to track your Percentage to Completion. Come up with some metrics. Concentrate on small tasks when progress is very difficult.*

Note: You can also try counting down to zero. If you are doing 10 reps of squats, count down 10, 9, 8, 7... until you reach zero. If you have 12 days of football camp, count down 12, 11, 10, 9... until the last day. We naturally use this strategy to count down time, but try applying it to other tasks as well.

Serenity Prayer – Focus on the Changeable

> "God grant me the serenity to accept the thing I cannot change, courage to change the things I can, and wisdom to know the difference."
> -Reinhold Niebuhr

This is time-tested stress-reduction technique that increases our problem-focus and mental tenacity. Remember that anxiety is linked to fear, and there is nothing more fearful than the unknown. That percentage of the puzzle that isn't up to you – the part outside your control – is a huge source of apprehension and breeder of doubt.

We don't like doubt. It is not a welcome guest. We don't like, "What if" questions that don't have obvious answers. That is why we concentrate on the here-and-now - the immediate task at hand - the things we have direct control over.

This method rests on the principle of Internal Locus of Control. Put the vast majority of your focus and efforts on what you can change, not what you can't. Put some Contingency Planning in place for uncontrollable variables, but don't dwell on them. Prepare possible ways to react then put it out of mind. Identify the elements that are out of your control and don't let them splinter your Focused Energy. Limit distractions. This produces a "can do" attitude.

You are in charge of your destiny - don't let anything tell you that you are not.

An actress preparing for an audition has no control over the ultimate choice the director makes. Maybe the director is looking for a certain "look", maybe the movie will end up getting scrapped, or maybe the part has already been promised to a relative. These things are out of her control, and dwelling on them does nothing but distract her. What the actress can do is know her lines well, look her best and perform her best. Focusing on those actions within her power to change is the successful strategy. Otherwise, "let the chips fall where they may."

You can't change the weather, you can't change your boss, you can't change your spouse, the economy, what people say about you or whether Punxatawny Phil sees his shadow – so don't slow yourself down thinking about it. Stay on fertile ground. Change yourself – your attitudes, beliefs, habits and actions.

List the aspects of your situation that are in your control and out of your control. Resolve to spend your time on the things you can change.

Count your Blessings

This is a simple way to increase your levels of optimism when negativity is swirling around you. The "bads" have a way of out-weighting the "goods" in our mind. We may have six things go right tomorrow morning and one thing go wrong, but you better believe that one wrong thing is the one that is going to take up the majority of our thoughts - if we let it. Once we stop and take a realistic look at the day, we feel much better about it. Whatever the situation, it's rarely as bad as our emotions tell us it is - and it could always be much, much worse.

When the going gets tough, the tough... count their blessings.

We tend to maximize our failures and minimize our successes. That is not productive. When we take a thorough and honest evaluation of the situation, it is usually much more optimistic than we realize.

List all the positive things that have happened recently. Think of all you have been given, everything going right, all the success you have enjoyed and all the progress you have made. Look forward to a triumphant future.

Refocus - Avoid Distraction

Most days we feel like an octopus, with each of our 8 arms being pulled in a different direction. Or like a mother bird with one worm to give and a dozen squawking hungry mouths all pleading for our attention. Point being, life is full of distractions.

It's a given, turbulence and confusion are going to be there. They are not the enemy - they are simply the field on which we play. It's very easy to lose sight of our objectives in the melee, but we employ powerful methods to maintain and refocus our efforts.

Those who accomplish the most are simply those who are best at filtering and prioritizing. Think of it like a toddler's block set – we just have to take the pieces handed to us daily, recognize the shapes and put each one through the correct hole.

Physical Reminders

First, remind yourself of your goal. Bring your V-Day image to mind often, especially under duress. This is the magnet that pulls you towards triumph. It is our light at the end of the tunnel. If possible, keep a physical reminder of your goal. Boxers have been known to keep a picture of their adversary on prominent display to "keep your eyes on the prize".

A salesperson may post a clipping of a yacht she or he wants to buy; a high school football player can keep a t-shirt from the school he wants to get a scholarship to; a beauty pageant contestant could have a tiara sitting on her nightstand; and an inventor might make the blueprint of his or her invention a computer background.

When the going gets tough, the tough... focus on V-Day.

Whatever you can find – a song, a picture, an object - that will keep your attention planted firmly on your goal, use it. And if people laugh at you, laugh with them. Your accomplishments will speak for themselves. Remember the SAS motto, "Who dares, wins."

> *Decide on some physical reminders of your goals that will instantly bring your V-Day image to mind.*

Incorporate them into your routine in an unavoidable way.

Checklists

Second, make a checklist and prioritize your activities. When we have too many tasks on our plate we feel overwhelmed and negative emotions set in. The Warning System is activated. We need to regain a feeling of comfortable control.

When the going gets tough, the tough... make a checklist.

So, write down all the pressing short-term tasks on your mind. Make a to-do list. Include components related to your goals. Then, prioritize. Start with the urgent survival sort of items – doctor's appointments, clothing the kids, paying the bills. Break the big tasks into chunks. Be political – do enough to keep as many people as possible happy while taking care of yourself and your own needs – including goal attainment. Find a slot to put each block into, then relax. You have a plan, now all you have to do is execute.

> *Create a checklist of all near-term duties and responsibilities. Balance others' needs as best you can while leaving room for your own needs – including your goals and dreams.*

Rest

There is a mathematical limit to our output. You intake a number of calories, your body can digest and absorb a certain amount of nutrients, and you can expend a certain amount of energy. Just like a car can over-heat and G-Forces begin to pull a plane apart, we each have a personal limit to our production.

We want to function close to those limits to achieve maximum efficiency, but if we find that we have over-stepped our boundaries, we have to rest. In bodybuilding the biggest muscle growth is made when you incrementally overload the muscular network, but if you train too hard you enter exhaustion and the muscle fibers break down instead of building up. This is when injuries occur. When you think that you have pushed yourself beyond healthy growth into the zone of exhaustion, take a break.

Sometimes we have to pass our limits before we know them.

Likewise, it is possible to reach a plateau with your efforts, in which increased output only brings marginal benefit – the law of diminishing returns. If you feel like you are beating your head against the wall and getting nowhere, take a breather, clear your mind, allow your system to regenerate itself, and once refreshed return to the fray with redoubled effort.

Don't let yourself sit in a quagmire, spinning your tires. Regroup, recover, then press forward. But this is the key – always, always, *always* have a specific plan and time frame for re-starting your efforts. This prevents your mind from playing any tricks on you. It ensures a break remains a break, and doesn't become permanent.

What we do not want is to slow down and have trouble speeding up again. What we do want is to have a set-time to relax, recuperate, and then begin again with increased effort and productivity. Don't think of it as a stop at a rest area as you drive cross country on the interstate. There is no gain in that. Think of it as a pit stop on a racetrack – you got a full tank of gas, fresh tires, adjusted aerodynamics and are ready to start putting down your fastest laps.

Taking a break from your goals is sometimes necessary but is always dangerous. It's the first step that is often the hardest. You are pausing your momentum, and remember that "an object at rest stays at rest." If you are feeling burnt out, put it on hold and do something to rejuvenate yourself – go to a movie, get a massage, go on vacation, spend a week doing something different, whatever you need – but before you take your holiday you need to make a very specific determination of when and how you will pick the trail back up.

> *If you are at a point of exhaustion, decide on a way to renew your mind and body. Before you take the break, write down exactly when and how you will come back to your goals. Include a new First Step.*

Positive Self Talk

"If you think you can, or you think you can't... either way you're right."
-Henry Ford

Here is an enlightening exercise: find a 10 minute block during your day and record all of your thoughts. Just write down (or talk out loud with a recorder going) and document what goes through your mind – stream of consciousness style.

Once you stop feeling silly, read it as if it is a script for a movie. You are likely to notice that we all talk to ourselves - just most of us have the presence of mind not to do it out loud. This is our internal dialogue, the conversation that is going on most of our waking hours. We say dozens of words to ourselves every minute of every day. And the odd part is, unless we pay attention, we are hardly aware of it - which is the reason for the meditation and awareness techniques we have implemented.

Another way to phrase this is "monkey mind". This Buddhist term refers to the stream of unconscious thoughts we have that are largely the result of the body's Warning System.

These are the voices of distraction, confusion, fear and reluctance that provide resistance to difficult efforts – negative self-talk. The term is often used in military training to refer to your body's attempt to make the mind quit under exhaustion: "Don't let your monkey mind tell you what to do."

Think of your internal dialogue as a blackboard or bathroom wall that every part of your mind and body can come up to and write on - a mini-democracy, where voices from every corner come to plead their case (and debate). This is where the Emotional Tug of War takes place, in addition to the more mundane thoughts like, "man, I'm hungry", "gross, its humid today," or "those are cute shoes. I wonder where she got them?"

Our concern here is with those times of extreme duress - those moments of truth - when we have the classic angel on one shoulder telling us to go on and a devil on the other telling us to quit. These are the pivotal times we need to tip the balance in favor of optimism and win the democratic vote in favor of continuing towards our goals. We accomplish this control of the internal dialogue through Positive Self Talk.

> **Positive Self Talk** – using short expressions of optimism and belief to increase motivation and push out negative thoughts; personal slogans to raise our spirits; phrases to increase emotional control

We all remember the story of the train who repeated, "I think I can, I think I can" as he made his way up the hill. It's a children's story, but the principle is spot-on. **You are what you think.** If you make your thoughts determined, positive ones, you will perform likewise. This is a defining characteristic of mental toughness.

Think of it as self-coaching. You may already have some mantras that you repeat to yourself in times of difficulty. If not, think of the way you cheer on your sports team or your kids at their games – this is what you are going to do, cheer yourself on. Chances are you are familiar with the Lance Armstrong slogan, "Live Strong." Here are some other sample mood elevators:

"This isn't so bad"

"Break through"

"Push it"

"I refuse to quit"

"You can't break me"

"Live the dream"

"Dig deep"

"Come on now, get serious"

"You gotta want it"

"No time like the present"

"No pain no gain"

"Let's rock'n roll"

"It's yours for the taking"

"No regrets"

"It's a beautiful day"

"Another day another dollar"

"Keep swinging"

If these sound like platitudes you might hear in a boxing club, on a football field or inside the training room of a high-pressure sales organization, you might be right. Put any stereotypes and prejudices aside, this is an effective habit of high achieving people. Mix them in with V-Day images for a synergistically potent combination.

Case study: Ronnie Coleman is the premier bodybuilder of our time. He set the world record with 8 consecutive Mr. Olympia victories (1998-2005). He has received the nickname "Mr. Relentless" for his work ethic, which has garnered almost as much fame as his mountain-sized biceps. It's his endless optimism and upbeat attitude that has made him a fan favorite, and has spawned dozens of YouTube video tributes. They are worth watching, both for his freakish muscle size, his gargantuan strength, and for his effective use of Positive Self Talk. Barely a second goes by that he is not keeping his confidence high by using his signature phrases, "Light weight, light weight!", "Yeah buddy!", "Nuttin to it but to do it!", and "Nuttin but a peanut!", which he constantly says in between sets and while squatting 800 pounds or leg pressing 2,000 pounds. His ability to maintain motivation during intense workouts with astronomical weight is truly amazing, and perfectly balanced with doses of humility after he finishes, panting, "Dang, that was heavy." He is a true master of mental toughness.

As soon as you feel negative thoughts entering your mind, think, "Stop!" or "Get behind me satan!" and repeat your own motivational phrase, "You're a machine!"

It's a way to control internal dialogue, win the Emotional Tug of War, keep the Warning System in check, boost confidence and burst through limitation barriers. This is sometimes referred to as "getting psyched". It's something very common to hear from external sources such as political leaders, supervisors, coaches, teachers and other motivators, and it is just as effective coming from an internal source - yourself.

Come up with a few personal slogans to boost your mood and increase intensity. Start inserting them into your internal dialogue during fatigue.

Be Led By Example

"Let us stand on the shoulders of giants."

Compare yourself to others. Find a role model that you would like to emulate and use it as a reference point. "What would Gen. Patton do in this situation?" "What would Peyton Manning do in this situation?" "How would a great salesperson react to this?" "How would Oprah handle this?" "What would Julia Child do?" "What would Jack Welch's next step be?"

This comparison can be to a real person or a fictitious, idealized person – what would a Fortune 500 CEO do, an Army Ranger, a Ritz Carlton manager, an NFL coach, etc.

Think of people you know (friends, relatives, associates), contemporary or historical figures, or the perfect example in your field – "a good father", "a good manager", "a top lawyer". Pick someone who defines excellence for you. We want to create a model for comparison. We want to copy excellence.

Then, when you encounter a friction-point and feel doubt or confusion taking grip, think, "What would [role model] do here?" "What advice would [role model] give me?" "How would [role model] proceed?" Aristotle was first to point out that it is by practicing the excellence of others that we gain

111

excellence ourselves. By mimicking the actions of great people we become great ourselves. Foggy situations have a way of becoming clear when we consider them from the perspective of someone else, especially someone who has already achieved excellence.

> *Pick a role model of excellence in your area of effort. Begin comparing yourself to that person. Measure yourself by this standard. Decide how your role model would act and follow that example.*

If-Then Statements

This is an easy way to amplify behavior change and habit forming effectiveness. What we are doing is mimicking the way the mind learns and creates rules for our daily reactions. Exploiting the brain's internal logic will help us build will power and mental fortitude.

Empirical learning is learning from experience. For instance, a child touches a hot pan and experiences the sensation of a burn. The child's mind remembers: *If* there is a pan on the stove, *then* I should not touch it. The logic sentence is, "If A (pan on stove), then B (do not touch). This is a contingency, and it is one of the brain's most basic methods for programming information. When the brain is presented with the stimulus (the "If") it produces an automatic connection to the response (the "Then").

This sounds elementary - however studies have shown people using If-Then statements for specific behavior modification have more than double the success rates than those who don't.

There is just something about the logic of an If-Then that penetrates more deeply into our minds. It seems more formal, more like a rule. It commands obedience. For instance, rather than saying, "I'm going to stop eating carbohydrate-heavy foods after 6PM", we decide, "*If* it is after 6PM, *then* I will not eat carbohydrate-heavy foods."

This "If" could be a time (If its Tuesday 6AM, then I'll take the trash out), place (If I am in the board room, then I will not mention expenses) or occasion (If my I'm offered a drink, then I'll have a Coke instead). And the "then" is the habit or behavior you want to build.

It seems like a small difference, but try it and see for yourself. Understand your brain and the way it integrates and uses information - then harness its latent power.

> *Think of 3 habits you want to form or behavior you want to change. Formulate them into If-Then statements. Reread the statements once daily until they become personal rules.*

Smile at the pain - Literally

We generally think of body language - our posture and facial expressions - as a byproduct of our emotions. If we feel sad, we cry. If we are happy, we smile. If we are angry, we frown. If we are impatient, we tap our fingers. The attitude of our mind transmits through the nervous system to our facial muscles and body.

Body language is the external physical manifestation of internal thoughts and attitudes. You are seeing on the outside what a person is feeling on the inside. That is the general assumption, but it is only half the story.

Here is the overlooked truth we can exploit to our advantage: **Body Language goes both ways. Your mind affects your body, but your body also affects your mind.**

Try it. Spend an hour tomorrow walking around with a frown on your face. Tense your facial muscles, clench your jaw and lower your chin just slightly. Make your hands into a fist. A few minutes into it you will notice a similar change in your attitude – you will begin to feel irritated, judge others more harshly and in general develop a negative, aggressive outlook. Likewise, spend a few minutes resting your head in your hand and you will start to feel sleepy. Cross your arms during a presentation and notice how your thoughts are more defensive and less agreeable.

We are not trying to turn into Oscar the Grouch, just to show a principle. The same rule holds for positive body language. Stand up in your office, put your hands on your hips and stick your chest out in your best Superman pose. Lift your chin with an air of confidence, now feel that confidence enter into you.

Experienced lecturers and salespeople are adept at using body language cues to spot those members of an audience who are drifting away from them. They spot boredom, negativity, defensiveness and hostility and will ask those people a question to get them back on their "side". Often at the beginning of such events you are given food or items such as pens. This is more than just a goodwill gesture, it is an attempt to get you to use your hands to open up your body language so that you will be more receptive to the message.

Have you ever seen a person in an argument (or a parent with a child) take the partner by the hands, thereby uncrossing the arms, and stoop down into the person's field of view (raising the partner's eyes and chin)? This is a subconscious effort to open the person's body language so he or she will receive our words. We can use body language to open the doors to the mind.

When the going gets tough, the tough... smile.

We want to learn to do the same thing to ourselves. When you feel negativity coming on and you want to reverse the thoughts, reverse the body first. When you are feeling stress and pain accumulate, smile. Smile at the pain – literally.

The smile is a powerful indicator of optimism and wellness. Our brain is encoded to associate that particular set of muscle contractions with positive emotions and thoughts. Either the emotions can come first, or the smile can come first and the emotions second. Smiling is associated with a good sense of humor, and they are both strongly correlated with high levels of goal attainment and mental toughness. Cultivate the ability to laugh at irony and smile in times of difficulty – it will boost your energy and increase your self-confidence.

You might be in the middle of a workout wincing with muscle fatigue, at a meeting frustrated that your advice is not being heeded, in an argument with your spouse, or trying to get a bolt under your sink to line up correctly – whatever the situation – force yourself to smile. Mix in a V-Day image or positive slogan, take a deep breath and smile for a second. If you take a bathroom break, do it in the mirror. Straighten up your posture, stand tall and bold, and smile with optimism. It's rarely as bad as it seems, and your muscles will tell your mind, "It's gonna be alright, we're gonna whip this thing." It's virtually impossible to feel defeated when you are smiling.

> *Become aware of your body language. Read a book about it if you get the chance. Become aware of your posture and facial expression. When you feel dark clouds closing in, smile.*

Case Study: Use of Botox has been argued as an effective cure for depression. Why? David Havas has done research on Botox users that suggests the inability to frown after treatment (when muscles are temporarily paralyzed) hampers our ability to feel anger and sadness. Halt the sadness muscles, halt the sadness. The exact effectiveness is still under debate, but the point is clear – our facial expressions, and our body language, are strong influencers of our emotional state. Stay smiling, stay positive.

Personal Soundtrack - Use Music to Elevate Mood

Music has a potent ability to elicit emotions and impact mood. A song can immediately take us to a certain time and place, or put us in a very specific mental state.

Directors regularly use music to set a scene and define a character. Start watching movies and pay attention to the use of music – imagine how much would be missing if the background scores and soundtracks were cut out.

Music is one more weapon in our arsenal to control the Warning System and win the Emotional Tug of War. It can instantly elevate your mood, increase energy levels and provide effective distraction to break through pain barriers and friction points. Studies have shown that listening to upbeat music during exercise can make you lift harder and run further. But we shouldn't use this powerful tool just for exercise.

Come up with some theme songs to listen to before making sales calls, on the way to and from work, before giving presentations, while writing a business plan (probably something classical for background) or anytime throughout the day. Work it into your schedule at appropriate times. It will become a cue to concentrate on a specific task and make the hours of labor pass by more quickly. Think of music as an energy drink for your emotional state.

Create a playlist of songs that will become a soundtrack to your goals. Start using it to prime your psyche and increase stamina.

Nothing Lasts Forever

"Tough times never last, but tough people do."
-Robert H. Schuller

When you are in a friction point and progress is difficult, remember that nothing lasts forever. This phase will pass. Think of how different things will be a month from now, a year from now, five years from now.

Think of sports dynasties – teams that dominated one decade often don't make the playoffs the next decade. Remember a low point in your life, and how it eventually turned towards the positive. Sooner or later, a new king is crowned. The Cold War eventually ended, grievous wounds fade to scars, cities are rebuilt, broken hearts love again, and the Red Sox finally won a World Series. Your infant will someday let you sleep through the night, that annoying song will stop playing on the radio. Your enemy will eventually run out of bullets; you will finish this workout and be in the refreshing shower soon.

Whatever the current situation is, it won't last. It's just a phase. If you are under stress, suffering, feeling pain, ride out the storm. Keep plugging away and know that there is a future coming and relief is only a matter of time. Persist.

Write down a situation that is causing you duress. Envision the future when this has been resolved and things are different. Stay focused on that future and keep working.

"This too will pass."
-Proverb

Handling Setbacks

> "I am not discouraged because every wrong attempt
> discouraged is another step forward."
> -Thomas Edison

Setbacks will happen. Everyone falls off the wagon at some point. Besides exhaustion, there are delays, miscalculations, and the plain old unexpected. We have cultivated an attitude that can react with Fluid Adaptation to change while maintaining maximum momentum and Focused Energy. We will now outline a method for quick recovery and optimum benefit from setbacks:

1. Debriefing

This is the "what". What happened, how, and why? Look for root causes. Was it something foreseeable, something avoidable? Was there a critical moment or decision?

Example: You are an ice-road trucker and got stuck going up a long incline. Did you have proper maps and knowledge of the terrain? Was your truck loaded correctly and outfitted with the best tires, chains etc.? What gearing did you use, how did you apply the throttle, how did you react when you began to experience loss of traction?

2. Lessons Learned

> "Results? Why man, I have gotten a lot of of results. I know
> 50,000 things that won't work."
> -Thomas Edison

What are your take-aways? What could have been done differently? What did I overlook? Is there a principle that I have discovered? Look for nuggets of wisdom and insights to tighten the focus of your efforts going forward. Any experience you learn from can become a good experience.

Example: You realize you did not map your route thoroughly enough before starting and did not see the incline approaching through the snow squalls until too late. The garage had your tire pressure a little high which may have robbed you of some traction. If you had been in a higher gear the power output would have been smoother and less likely to spin. And your gut reaction to floor the throttle likely accelerated the spinning tires and dug divots in the ice.

3. Resolutions

Turn your lessons into actionable resolutions. What will I change in my approach? How can my strategies be tweaked? How can setbacks be avoided or minimized? Create rules and norms for the future.

Example: Always map your route and note areas where you will need caution so you have advanced warning. Double check your tire pressure before leaving during extreme conditions. Accelerate for inclines as early as possible while still on level and switch to higher gear as you begin the incline. Maintain even throttle control during traction loss.

4. Execute

Incorporate your new experiential knowledge into your plans and use it. Make reminders until your resolutions become automatic. Create a new First Step if one is needed to get you back on track. Don't make the same mistake twice. Clear your mind and put the past behind you. You have learned and become stronger. Track your future success in these areas and celebrate your growth.

"The only way to lose is to quit trying"

"Failure folds to persistence"

Examples

Note: Do not feel that you need to use every one of these methods every day. Some fit one person's personality better than others; some fit better with particular goals than others. Understand them all, experiment with them all. Rotate them in and periodically review the chapter for a tactic you haven't used in awhile. Rely on the techniques that feel most natural and you find most effective as your primary weapons.

Example 1: Ivy League University

F.A.C.E.
Face Facts
You didn't get into your top choice school.

Accept Situation
Not getting in is the New Normal. It is the new situation and won't change without action.

Consider Options
Go to second choice school or go to junior college one year and reapply.

Execute
Enroll at junior college and set up new action plan to reapply successfully.

Micro Visualization
Before taking the SAT, spend five minutes visualizing your actions. Imagine yourself successfully answering the questions, getting done with some time to spare, feeling confident as you make your choices and getting back excellent results.

Micro Goals
Divide and Conquer
When studying, concentrate on reading just one more page at a time.

Percentage to Completion
Calculate how many math problems you have for homework. Keep track of your percentage to completion as you finish each problem.

Serenity Prayer
You can't influence the admission board. But you can get the highest grades and best recommendations possible.

Count Your Blessings
Be glad you have the mental faculties to attend a good college and the means to pay for college.

Physical Reminders
Get a list of the top 10 schools ranking and post it outside your notebook.

Checklist
Tomorrow: study for geography exam 45 minutes; attend soccer practice; ask Mr. Smith to write a recommendation

Rest
Take a Saturday off, sleep in and relax. Continue on Sunday with writing a page of one college admission essay.

Positive Self Talk
"Let's get serious". Say during studying and practicing SAT to keep focus.

Be Led By Example
What would an Ivy League student do? He or she would study another 20 minutes...

If-Then Rules
If it's Thursday, then I will be at the Student Council meeting.

Smile at the Pain
While memorizing words for the SAT, smile periodically to delay fatigue.

Music
Play Mozart in the background while studying.

Nothing Lasts Forever
You won't always have the SAT hanging over your head. Once you are enrolled in college, all you will have to do is attend to your classes.

Handling Setbacks
Debriefing
You got a low score in the math section of the SAT.

Lessons Learned
You are weak in Algebra.

Resolutions
Get some tutoring from your math teacher.

Execute
Set up a schedule for tutoring.

Example 2: Army Ranger

F.A.C.E.
Face Facts
It has begun raining and you still have 10 miles to march.

Accept Situation
It is difficult and uncomfortable, but you will do it anyway.

Consider Options
Stop and waterproof yourself or continue and finish fast.

Execute

Waterproof to prevent illness. Then continue.

Micro Visualization
You are about to begin the 5 mile run. Visualize yourself running, your legs pumping in rhythm, you lungs taking deep breaths. Imagine the pain and fatigue coming on, but see yourself continuing at a fast pace anyway, passing several other candidates and sprinting across the finish line with your best time yet.

Micro Goals
Divide and Conquer
When you are having extreme fatigue, do just five more push-ups. Then three more. Then one more. Then one more...

Percentage to Completion
When you have to run 5 miles, track each mile as a percentage of the whole. First mile is twenty percent done. Third mile is past half way...

Serenity Prayer
You can't change the weather, but you can be prepared for the right gear. You can't choose your squad members, but you can inspire them to do their best.

Count Your Blessings
You are well fed, have no injuries or blisters, you are training with the best soldiers in the Army.

Physical Reminders
Cut out a picture of the Ranger Tab and tape it under your hat.

Checklist
Tomorrow: take ASVAB practice test; read Ranger Creed twice; run 3 miles.

Rest

Your legs are aching worse than usual. Take three days off. Wednesday you will continue progress with a full-body weightlifting session and 10 x 100m sprints.

Positive Self Talk
"Break through." While running and doing push-ups.

Be Led by Example
An Army Ranger. How would a Ranger react to this?

If-Then Rules
If I just woke up, then I will shave.

Smile at the Pain
When you are in the middle of a rucksack march or feeling drowsy, smile and show positive body language.

Music
Play classic rock while working out on an MP3 player.

Nothing Lasts Forever
Basic training will eventually end. You will eventually be doing more interesting training.

Setbacks
Debriefing
You missed your target time for the 2-mile run.

Lessons Learned
If you push the pace too much in the first mile you run out of energy.

Resolutions
Keep an even pace till the last two laps of the second mile.

Execute
Pace yourself on the next run and keep a steady pace.

Example 3: Business Owner

F.A.C.E.
Face Facts
Your current curling irons won't work for the new popular hairstyle.

Accept Situation
The curling irons are outdated, a paradigm shift has happened in curler technology.

Consider Options
Refer people wanting this hairstyle to a competitor, convince them to not get the hairstyle, or buy new curlers.

Execute
It seems like a fad that won't last, we will recommend a different hairstyle or refer customers.

Micro Visualization
You have a very influential client coming in. Visualize how the appointment will go. Imagine yourself greeting her, what you will say and do, how the washing will go, what you will say and do as you cut and style her hair. Watch yourself making precise cuts and see the finished product, feel the pride and relief as you make a perfect new style for this valuable patron.

Micro Goals
Divide and Conquer
When you are cutting hair and the salon s backed up, just concentrate on finishing the person in front of you. Just cut one person at a time.

Percentage to Completion
Break your business plan up into chapters. Count your percentage done as you complete each section and get closer to completion.

Serenity Prayer
You can't convince people what hairstyle they should get to look their best and make you look good, but you can give them exactly what they ask for so that they speak highly of you to friends.

Count Your Blessings
You have a family supporting you, you write well, you have talent for salon skills and you have a look that makes you approachable.

Physical Reminders
Draw a rough sketch of the logo you want to use for your business. Put it on the refrigerator so you see it every day.

Checklist
This week: exam on manicures Tuesday; exercise class at 7 every night; get the oil changed Wednesday; attend trade show on Saturday.

Rest
Your hands are tired from cutting hair and giving pedicures at class. Take the week in between semesters off and do other things you enjoy. Next Monday you will give two friends a trim and read the first chapter of your text for the next class.

Positive Self Talk
"I can do this thing." Repeated while studying and working.

Be Led By Example
Your Aunt Bettie. She owns her own law firm and is a strong, competent woman. What would Bettie tell me to do?

If-Then Rules
If I have extra money left over at the month's end, then I will use it to pay off debt.

Smile at the Pain
When people criticize your business plan and question your projected numbers, smile.

Music
Put on your favorite Top 40 station in your salon to keep everyone in an upbeat mood.

Nothing Lasts Forever
The shop build-out and set up seems tedious and never ending. So many small details. Remember that most of these things you set up once and never move - soon it will be running like clockwork.

Handling Setbacks
Debriefing
Your sales dipped last month.

Lessons Learned
Giving a 50% off coupon didn't bring new people in, it just gave a break to repeat customers.

Resolutions
Give coupons only when it will bring in new customers.

Execute
Give repeat customers a coupon that gives them 25% off when they bring in a friend.

Step 5: Celebrate Success – Small and Large

"All work and no play makes Jack a dull boy."

There is simply no point to a successful life if we don't take the time to savor it. Don't work for work's sake – work to live. It's like making a gourmet meal for your family and not sitting down to take a bite. If you don't take time to "smell the roses" and unwind a bit, you will eventually burn out, and overall you will not achieve as much.

As we are striving, with our nose to the grindstone, we have a tendency to become myopic – our field of vision closes in and we become near sighted. We want to stay focused, for sure, but it is also very healthy to pause and take time to realize how far we have come, give thanks, and enjoy a little pat on the back. Take in the scenery and savor the moment.

Regular periods of reflection and celebration do not slow our progress, rather they increase our confidence and pride (the good kind) – and generally increase our level of satisfaction in life.

Humans like praise. We like to know we've done a good job, even when we are telling ourselves.

We have smaller and larger goals, and our celebrations should have similar proportions. We often forget to reward ourselves for our small victories. If you have a great workout and break through a strength or endurance barrier, reward yourself with a piece of cake for dessert. Keep a cookie jar or bottle of bubble bath. Play an upbeat song driving home with an air of triumph. If you have a great week of sales, have a nice dinner at a favorite restaurant.

When possible, include your friends, family, spouse, battle buddy or mentor in your daily successes – they are likely to enjoy your enthusiasm and you are likely to enjoy their support.

If you hit a big Milestone, invite some people for a get-together. You don't have to brag about yourself or even mention specifically the reason for the celebration, just say you hit some goals and feel like having a fun evening. Failing to recognize our success is a reason many people lose motivation, so always take a little time to adjust your laurels and give thanks.

Review Progress Regularly

This is the cousin of "Treasure what you Measure". Since you are logging your steps towards your goals, it is easy to do a quick review to see how far you have come. If you want to get intense about it you can plot a graph to see your incremental gains across time, but usually a glance-over analysis is sufficient.

Review often enough to keep your focus, but not so often as to produce extra anxiety. Find a system that works and make it consistent. Daily, weekly, monthly – it depends on the goal. But do set a schedule for gauging your advancement and stick to it. As with everything, be systematic and specific.

By doing so you will create a "snowball effect" – the more you accomplish, the more you grow, the bigger the momentum of energy becomes. And the bigger it becomes, the harder it becomes to knock you off course. Expect your progress to build exponentially and for the methods outlined in this chapter to become more and more automatic. You are becoming an unstoppable, invincible mechanism of achievement.

Set a schedule for analyzing your progress. Mark it on a calendar if it helps. Be consistent.

Debrief and Tweak

As you hit Milestones, go through the Debriefing process. Do a quick after-action review. What worked? What could have been done better? What areas are you excelling in? Where could you use some extra effort?

Even A-list Hollywood actors and actresses go back and take acting lessons, mix it up with some theatre exposure or brush up on dialect training. Personal trainers have to take a certain number of courses to keep their certification current. Most Fortune 500 CEOs will benefit from taking some lessons in the newest version of Excel.

Don't be shy to go back to some of your Skills to freshen up or fill in the gaps. Always be improving. Up your game. Review your Relaxation Techniques. Add some new willpower building exercises. Increase your knowledge. Tweak your plan of attack, add or subtract some strategies. Oil the machine. Refine the process. You will increase your efficiency and effectiveness. And the next Milestone will come that much sooner.

When you reach Milestones, do a quick assessment. Review your actions and look for one or two areas to fine-tune. Add them to your future plans.

Look in the Mirror

You are evolving and that's great. If your tastes change, that's fine. A lot of life is narrowing down what you do *not* want to do. And sometimes experience is the only way to do it. It's not just about the doors you open, but the doors you close as well.

So if you find out that your career or endeavor no longer fulfills you, that's fine. Adjust. Very few of us are born knowing exactly what we want to do and who we want to be. Happy, healthy individuals are those who have a strong sense of purpose and a feeling of usefulness. But there is some element of trial-and-error to this process.

As you learn more about yourself, you may come to new conclusions. There is nothing wrong with switching directions as long as you keep moving forward. **What's most important is having the courage to evaluate yourself with honesty and integrity while maintaining a trajectory of growth.**

> *Take 5 minutes and look at yourself in the mirror. What do you see? Are your actions consistent with your beliefs? Are you growing in the right direction? Does the look in your eyes match the thoughts in your mind?*

Do this every few months. Think of it as a gut check. If you have an intuition that there is consistency in your thoughts, words and deeds, and this is reflected back at you, that's what you want. If you can look at that person, and with honest appraisal, accepting faults and strengths alike, gain a feeling of optimism - excellent. You are a strong, driven, motivated, mentally strong individual with a sense of purpose and you will what you put your mind to.

No Such Thing as Neutral

"Everybody wants to know what I'm on. What am I on? I'm on my bike busting my ass six hours a day. What are you on? "
– Lance Armstrong

Like a ball on an incline, we are either moving up or moving down, but there is no such thing as staying still. You are either making ground or losing ground, progressing or digressing. Your mind is positive or your mind is negative.

Either you act, or things act on you. You move, or you are moved. There is never a static moment. This is a principle that Medieval monks used to conceptualize their striving towards holiness – there is no such thing as stagnant – you are either moving forward or moving backwards.

Even when you rest, you are resting with the purpose of increased future efforts. You know how you will continue on. Your rest is building momentum. Because of your internal motivation, you are never motionless. Your emotions - your committed resolve and sense of purpose - are always pulling you towards the finish.

"Darkness cannot exist in the presence of light."

There is no such thing as standing still. You are on an incline; you are climbing a peak. If you aren't moving ahead, you are planning ahead. If you aren't acting, you are preparing. There is no neutrality. There is no parking brake. There is gravity pulling you down and your invincible spirit pushing you up. Keep V-Day in mind and keep moving. Remind yourself of this during your moments of reflection.

Reward Yourself for Success

You may resist, but do it. We give puppies "treats", we give toddlers "prizes", and we should give ourselves rewards as well. Reward reinforces our sense of progress and provides a subtle distraction during the distress - giving you something to symbolically look forward to that pulls your mind above the short-term discomfort.

Training as a competitive MMA fighter, I got in the habit of going to a convenience store after every practice and getting a pint of chocolate milk. My body craved the sugar and protein to rebuild the exhausted muscles, and the sensation was very satisfying. It got to the point that I actually looked forward to the grueling 3 hour long training sessions just because I knew the triumphant swilling of 32 ounces of chocolate milk was waiting for me at the end. The harder I trained and the more I sweated, the better the milk tasted. It turned into daily mini-celebrations of success. For me, this solidified the power of reward.

Maybe you do something as simple as get a coffee or put in a stick of gum every time you make a sale, or watch a half-hour of television after you write a page of your business plan. Get a new outfit every time you lose another 5 pounds, spend a day at the beach every time you ace a test, or buy a nice watch every time you get a promotion. It's popping a champagne bottle on a miniature scale – some little prize to take your mind off the work itself and add a little stress-reducing pleasure to your day.

> *Write down some ways you will reward yourself for your efforts, large and small. Link specific rewards to specific actions.*

Trophies - Build on Success

Trophies are the mementos of our accomplishments. Plaques, diplomas, pictures, souvenirs – rather than stuff them away in closets, put them on display. Adorn your walls, desk, and mantelpiece – surround yourself with reminders of your accomplishments.

> "Been there, done that."

It will build a foundation of self-confidence and in moments of doubt provide proof positive of your mental toughness, tenacity, and unstoppable ability to reach your goals. These are constant reminders of how far you have come and how much you are capable of. It reinforces belief and fosters satisfaction. Savor your victories. Cherish your memories.

Self-Monitoring

Self-Monitoring is the process of systematically observing and recording one's own behavior and includes all the oversight you have been doing to achieve your goals. We built a detailed plan with many specific actions to follow and in the beginning you will have to look back at your notes often to drive the points home and stay on target. You will have to break habits and patterns of thinking and form new ones. These are the growing pains of mental toughness, the birthing pains of achievement.

Mental toughness is like learning to ride a bike. The techniques will stop being conscious efforts and become automatic responses – you will move from practice to performance. As your brain structure grows and adapts, they will simply become part of your personality. As these methods become ingrained habits and we start making leaps of progress, as our abilities to stay focused and constantly adapt with no loss of energy become second nature, we have a tendency to trail off on our self-monitoring.

That's alright. Once you get in "the zone", you won't need to look at your progress charts as often, consult mentors as often, or think of your V-Day images as often. Your progress will become a systematic, unconscious force and you will approach the realm of Invincibility.

Your feeling of self-confidence and your overwhelming belief that you will succeed – a swagger – will be your clue that you can begin to trail off your self-monitoring. Your enjoyment of the process itself will rise. You have mastered the art of achievement. You can dispense with the training wheels.

Still, set-up a system of checks and balances to make sure your confidence does not get ahead of you. Never think that you are beyond the need for improvement. We started out with a tricycle and now we are on a race bike. It's natural that monitoring will become less frequent. But always retain a set schedule for Debriefing, progress reports and self-checks to make sure the hard work you have done in building momentum does not begin to lose steam over time.

You can move to monthly, bi-monthly or bi-yearly evaluations, but it's not recommended to space them any farther than a year. Think of it as maintenance on your car, a virus scan on your computer, getting an oil change or a check-up at the doctor. Even if everything feels great, it doesn't hurt to take a minute to look under the hood. Glance over the chapters for new insights. Review your Mega Goals, your Sub-Goals and Milestones, talk to mentors, look at possible skills training, go through your visualization of success, look in the mirror – seek techniques from you may have forgotten to use or any tweaks that can make the machine more efficient.

You have built a machine and put it in motion. You have tuned it from top to bottom. You have made it lean, mean and efficient. You have accelerated to top gear and put it on cruise control. Now you just continue with periodic maintenance to stay at the front of the race.

> *As you master mental toughness and hit your stride, set a long-term interval for self-monitoring. Make it no longer than a year. Perform a general analysis from top to bottom. Look for fresh insights and ongoing improvements. Celebrate your success.*

"It is not the critic who counts, not the man who points out how the strong man stumbled, or where the doer of deeds could have done better. The credit belongs to the man who is actually in the arena; whose face is marred by the dust and sweat and blood; who strives valiantly; who errs and comes short again and again; who knows the great enthusiasms, the great devotions and spends himself in a worthy course; who at the best, knows in the end the

triumph of high achievement, and who, at worst, if he fails, at least fails while daring greatly; so that his place shall never be with those cold and timid souls who know neither victory or defeat."
-Theodore Roosevelt, France 1910

Examples

Example 1: Ivy League University

Review Progress
Record your efforts on a daily and weekly basis. Review your progress at the end of each term.

Debrief and Tweak
Your studies don't seem efficient. Try flash cards and study groups.

Look at Yourself in the Mirror
You are becoming a great student and interesting person. Great!

Reward Yourself
Have cookies and milk every night after you finish your studies.

Trophies
Honor roll certificate, high school varsity letter, college diploma.

Self Regulate
Once you have become an elite student, analyze your achievement and celebrate twice a year, at the end of the semesters.

Example 2: Army Ranger

Review Progress
Track your exercise goals after every workout, review your progress weekly.

Debrief and Tweak
Your marksman scores aren't where you want them. Begin practicing muscle control exercises and ask instructor for help.

Look at Yourself in the Mirror
You define the properties of a Ranger. You are seeing the world. It's a great time to be alive!

Reward Yourself
Every time you take a minute off your five mile time, treat yourself to a steak dinner.

Trophies
Pictures from your graduating class from Ranger School, your uniform, souvenirs from countries you've visited.

Self Regulate
Once the pain and fatigue just become a background noise and you have great control over your Warning System, analyze your efforts, review other strategies and celebrate your efforts every time you come home on leave.

Example 3: Business Owner

Review Progress
Set your weekly goals for activity, do a bi-monthly evaluation of overall progress.

Debrief and Tweak
Your hair stylists are not taking on as many appointments per day as they could. Set a target number of appointments for them per month and include a bonus if they reach it.

Look at Yourself in the Mirror
You are independent and making good money, but you feel like your business owns you instead of you owning it. Decide to delegate more and spend a little less time "at the office".

Reward Yourself
Every month that you hit your profit goals, take your kids shopping and get a new pair of shoes for everyone.

Trophies
Hang the first dollar of revenue on the wall, cosmetology degree, pictures of the 100th customer, 1000th customer etc.

Self Regulate
Once you get in a good rhythm and have solid, reliable profits, have a thorough quarterly review of financials, celebrate with your staff, add a few techniques you haven't used in a while.

Appendix A: Current Research

a. Goal Setting

Among the benefits to goal setting found by researchers are, "(a) increases performance, (b) provides an unambiguous basis for judging success, (c) increases one's subjective well-being, (d) provides a sense of purpose, and (e) is a means for self-management." (Latham & Locke, 2006) A separate study on motivation found that tasks with high rewards also lead to an increase in focus and attention. (Veling & Aarts, 2010)

Latham, G.P., & Locke, E.A. (2006). Enhancing the Benefits and Overcoming the Pitfalls of Goal Setting. *Organizational Dynamics, 35,* 332-340.

Veling, H., & Aarts, H.(2010). Cueing task goals and earning money: Relatively high monetary rewards reduce failures to act on goals in a Stroop task. *Motivation and Emotion, 34,* 184-190.

b. Goals Should be Long-Term and Specific

To be effective, goals also need to be *long-term* and *specific.* A study in which subjects wrote down goals ranging in time from one week to lifetime found that, "a higher goal specificity and a longer future time perspective lead to greater persistence and satisfaction in the pursuit of more proximal goals." Further, "Analyses revealed that with increasing time range there is an increase in level of importance, effort, persistence, and satisfaction, and a decrease in conflict." Therefore, specific long-term goals increase our effectiveness in meeting shorter term sub-goals. (Zaleski, 1987)

Zaleski, Z. (1987). Behavioral effects of self-set goals for different time ranges. *International Journal of Psychology, 22,* 17.

c. Emotions Towards Goals

In addition to the goals themselves, the attitude of the individual towards the goals has been found to be a predictor of success. A study of the personality traits of eighty-nine college students was compared to their ability to reach goals over a one year period, revealing that, "goal attainment is predicted best by individuals' appraisals of their goals. Higher levels of commitment, motivation, positive emotion, self-efficacy, and perceived opportunity for success were associated with higher levels of goal attainment." So, in addition to setting goals that are difficult, long-term and specific, individuals should have an attitude towards their goals marked by *strong commitment, self-confidence, optimism,* and *belief.* (Stimson, 2010)

Stimson, T. (2010). The precursors and outcomes of goal choice and attainment. *The Sciences and Engineering, 71,* 1386.

d. Hope and Belief Predict Success

As goals are set, a wealth of emotion surrounds one's endeavor. The content of these emotions has been shown to predict our goal attainment over time. Specifically, "hopefulness positively predicted mastery and performance goals, whereas helplessness negatively predicted mastery goals. Mastery goals positively predicted enjoyment, which in turn positively predicted achievement, and negatively predicted boredom, which in turn negatively predicted achievement." This means that *hopefulness,* or *belief,* regarding our goals leads to success in subgoals and a feeling of enjoyment, which turns into long-term achievement, whereas hopelessness, or doubt, predicts lower achievement. So as goals are set, they should have an accompanying emotion of hope and belief to increase effect. (Daniels et Al., 2009)

Daniels, L.M., Stupinksy, R.H., Pekrun, R., Haynes, T.L., Perry, R.P., Newall, N.E. (2009). A longitudinal analysis of achievement goals: From affective antecedents to emotional effects and achievement outcomes. *Journal of Educational Psychology*, 948-963.

e. Commitment and Personal Values

In a separate study on factors of commitment from 1996, Lydon examined students' during an 8-week volunteer work project and found that, "students were more committed to the volunteer project if they reported that the project affirmed their personal values. The endings were more robust when students perceived the project as difficult and stressful." (Lydon, 1996, p. 191) The researchers theorized that, "A vivid personal vision may also reflect stronger, clear, and well-established values." (Masuda, Kane, Shoptaugh & Minor, 2010, p. 221) Personal projects that aligned with volunteers' core values predicted strong commitment to the goal. So personal vision, or high level goals, should reflect the individuals set of *cores desires and values* for life.

Lydon, J. (1996). Toward a theory of commitment. In C. Seligman, J. M. Olson, & M. P. Zanna (Eds.), *The psychology of values* (pp. 191–214). Mahwah, NJ: Erlbaum.

f. Goals should Be Difficult

Research has shown that goals should be *difficult*. A three year longitudinal study on the importance of difficulty in goal planning concluded, "Goal difficulty predicted change in all outcome criteria, that is, only adults who perceived their goals as difficult to reach also reported a change in positive and negative affect, job satisfaction, and subjective developmental success over a period of 3 years." (Weise & Freund, 2006) Likewise, the increase in self-confidence resulting from reached goals is much higher when the goals are more challenging. A study of the efforts of customers using frequent flyer programs found that success increased effort in future endeavors, but that, "the impact of success is significant only when the goal is challenging." (Dreze & Nunes, 2011) In other words, success breeds success, but only when we are striving towards difficult objectives.

Dreze, X. & Nunes, J.C. (2011). Recurring goals and learning: The impact of successful reward attainment on purchase behavior. *Journal of Marketing Research, 48,* 268-281.

Wiese, B.S. & Freund, A.M. (2005). Goal progress makes one happy, or does it? Longitudinal findings from the work domain. *Journal of Occupational and Organizational Psychology, 78,* 287-304.

g. Vision Imagery

The imagery that represents a goal is referred to as the individual's "vision". Research published in May 2010 outlines how certain characteristics of the personal vision have been proven to be factors of mental toughness. Specifically, an effective personal vision will, "indirectly relate with performance by stimulating the setting of difficult and specific proximal goals and by facilitating commitment to such goals." So, an effective vision will cause us to set difficult and specific subgoals and will increase our commitment – both of which will increase goal attainment. An effective vision was found to be one that is *challenging*, *vivid*, and high on *imagery*. It is noted, "A challenging vision will serve an energizing function by stimulating effort and persistence... Specifically, the extent to which a student's personal vision is challenging and vivid positively related with his or her attachment to semester task goals, unwillingness to lower these goals, and intended effort to attain these goals." (Masuda, Kane, Shoptaugh & Minor, 2010,) The research further states, "one's personal vision should be more compelling if it is high on imagery. A personal vision high on imagery defines in detail a clear and vivid picture of one's desired future." (Masuda, Kane, Shoptaugh & Minor, 2010)

Masuda, A., Kane, T.D., Shoptaugh, C.F., & Minor, K.A. (2010). The Role of a Vivid and Challenging Personal Vision in Goal Hierarchies. *Journal of Psychology, 3,* 221-242.

h. Effects of Sub-goals
A study was done by professors at Yale and University of Chicago to see if the pursuit of subgoals would be complementary to higher-level goals or whether the subgoals would become substitutes to one another and in essence compete for attention. The author states, "The self-regulation process often involves breaking an ongoing goal (e.g., keeping in shape) into many individual, constituent subgoals that monitor actual actions (e.g., eating healthy meals, going to the gym)." They then surveyed participants' attitudes towards subgoals and the effect this had on goal attainment. What they found was, "when people consider success on a single subgoal additional actions toward achieving a superordinate goal are seen as substitutes and are less likely to be pursued. In contrast, when people consider their commitment to a superordinate goal on the basis of initial success on a subgoal, additional actions toward achieving that goal may seem to be complementary and more likely to be pursued." This is to say that when subgoals are mentally linked to the higher goals, they increase the individual's actions toward the higher goal. Breaking down higher goals into linked subgoals is then considered another element of Mental Toughness and key to goal attainment. (Fishbach, Dhar & Zhang, 2006)

Fishbach, A., Dhar, R., & Zhang, Y. (2006). Subgoals as substitutes or complements: The role of goal accessibility. *Journal of Personality and Social Psychology,* 232-242.

i. Mental Toughness Training
An important question is not just what the elements and strategies of mental toughness are, but whether we can increase them through directed efforts. Evidence points

towards the affirmative, that mental toughness is something that can be taught, trained and developed. In a study of adolescent athletes in Australia, a single, two hour skills training session was given once per week over six weeks to two groups, "targeting self-regulation, arousal regulation, mental rehearsal, attentional control, self-efficacy, and ideal performance." The two groups attended sessions with similar but different curriculum, while a third group was kept as a control. The result was unanimous in favor of training, as "both intervention groups reported more positive changes in subjective ratings of mental toughness, resilience, and flow than the control group." The evidence shows that mental toughness and performance-oriented skills can be learned and developed. (Gucciardi, 2009)

Gucciardi, D.F. (2009). Evaluation of a mental toughness training program for youth-aged Australian footballers: I. A quantitative analysis. *Journal of Applied Sport Psychology, 21*, 307-323.

j. Exercise

Exercise has also been found to be an effective component of goal attainment. It has the ability to increase elements of mental toughness such as self-control, persistence and optimism. While it could be theorized that exercise becomes either a substitute for other goals or a competitor for time, research has shown the opposite to be true. A study published in the journal Psychology of Sport and Exercise in 2010 found, "Frequent exercisers had significantly higher levels of self-regulatory efficacy to manage concurrent, highly valued goals, greater persistence to achieve both types of goals, and perceived the pursuit of concurrent goals more positively than less frequent exercisers." So, the benefits of exercise in mental toughness carry over into the other facets of life as well. (Jung, 2010)

Jung, M.E. (2010). Concurrent management of exercise with other valued life goals: Comparison of frequent and less frequent exercisers. *Psychology of Sport and Exercise, 11,* 372-377.

k. Problem-Focused Coping

To achieve anything while striving in a challenging environment one needs to be able to react to stress and change, which is called coping. A 2009 study of 482 athletes aged 16-45 revealed that coping effectiveness was influenced by the specific coping strategies used; specifically, researchers found that, "higher levels of mental toughness were associated with more problem-focused coping, but less emotion-focused and avoidance coping." So, being able to use emotional control to focus coping on *problem solving* with less emotional distraction is an additional component of mental toughness. (Kaiseler & Polman, 2009)

Kaiseler, M., & Polman, R. (2009). Mental toughness, stress, stress appraisal, coping and coping effectiveness in sport. *Personality and Individual Differences, 47,* 728-733.

l. Self-Talk, Emotional Control, Relaxation Strategies

Just as there have been clearly identified and measured characteristics of mental toughness, there are specific strategies that have been associated with success in goal achievement. A 2010 study published in the European Journal of Sport Science revealed that, "self-talk, emotional control, and relaxation strategies were significantly and positively ($r = 0.26$ to 0.37, $P < 0.01$) related to mental toughness in both practice and competition." (Crust, 2010)

Crust, L. (2010). Mental toughness and athletes' use of psychological strategies. *European Journal of Sport Science, 10,* 43-51.

m. Humor

An unheralded component of mental toughness was identified in a study from the University of Western Ontario, which showed that humor contributes to mental toughness. This may be intuitive if we think about how someone with a "good sense of humor" is able to relieve the stress in a situation and "roll with the punches". Being able to see the irony in life is a good way to maintain a positive mental attitude. The study identified two positive and two negative humor styles; the positive styles were termed "affiliative", meaning humor with a sense of teamwork, and "self-enhancing"; the negative styles were "aggressive" and "self-defeating". Characteristics of humor style were compared with eight factors of mental toughness (Commitment, Control, Emotional Control, Control over Life, Confidence, Confidence in Abilities, Interpersonal Confidence, Challenge), with the conclusion that as positive humor styles increase, all eight measures of mental toughness increase as well. The old maxim "in every joke is a bit of truth" seems to hold. Those individuals with optimistic, self-confident jokes embody those traits, while individuals with cynical, defeatist humor patterns are lower in feelings of wellbeing and belief. (Veselka & Schermer, 2010)

Veselka, L., & Schermer, J.A. (2010). Laughter and resiliency: A behavioral genetic study of humor styles and mental toughness. *Twin Research and Human Genetics Oct, 13*, 442-449.

n. Embodied Cognition

Witt, J.K., Linkenauger, S.A., Bakdash, J.Z., Augustyn, J.S., Cook, A., Proffitt, D.R., (2009). The long road of pain: Chronic Pain increases perceived distance. *Experimental brain Research*, 192, 145-148.

Witt, J.K., Linkenauger, S.A., Bakdash, J.A., & Proffitt, D.R. (2008). Putting to a bigger hole: Golf performance relates to perceived size. *Psychonomic Bulletin & Review*, 15, 581-585.

Proffitt, D.R., Bhalla, M., Gossweiler, R., & Midgett, J. (1995). Perceiving geographical slant. *Psychonomic Bulletin & Review*, 2, 409-428.

Proffitt, D.R., Stefanucci, J., Banton, T., & Epstein, W. (2003). The role of effort in perceiving distance. *Psychological Science*, 14, 106-112.

o. Facial Muscles and Emotions

Havas, Glenberg, Gutowski, Lucarelli, & Davidson (2010). Cosmetic use of botulinum toxin affects processing of emotional language. *Psychological Science*.

Appendix B: Definitions

Divide and Conquer: the principle that victory is nothing more than a string of small wins; success is cumulative so the volume of wins matters more than their size; dividing larger goals into smaller and smaller increments as stress increases

Emotional Tug of War: the constant battle to maintain a healthy, productive mental state; controlling our thoughts and emotions to maintain positive vs. negative, optimism vs. pessimism, belief vs. doubt

Fluid Adaptation: the ability to quickly accept changes in conditions, react to new information and adjust seamlessly to minimize loss of momentum; capacity to maintain sense of homeostasis in unstable environment

Focused Energy: the ability of an individual to use time and resources effectively to achieve desired outcomes; the efficiency and precision of one's efforts; passion with purpose

Goal: an objective towards which we direct our efforts; a desired future state

Mega Goals: our highest level desires and achievements in life; the culmination of our striving; our life plan; vision of the desired future

Mental Toughness: the ability to overcome adversity in pursuit of an objective; the set of traits that enable one to maintain focused effort to achieve goals; strength of resolve under stress

Micro Goals: the smallest next step you can take towards you goal; the closest, most immediate success you can achieve with confidence

Milestones: definite increments leading closer to greater goals; sequential achievements

Percentage to Completion: keeping track of the fraction or percentage of the way to completion; working towards fractional parts of a goal as milestones that increases motivation and belief

Positive Self Talk: the process of using short expressions of optimism to increase motivation and push out negative thoughts; personal slogans to raise our spirits; phrases to increase emotional control

Sub-Goals: Short-term goals that are increments, components, building-blocks of our Mega Goals; stepping-stones on the way to higher accomplishments

Vacuum Thinking: dwelling on the negative, or empty, aspect of situations; being happy only with the ideal instead of the practical; concentrating on obstacle instead of solutions, seeing barriers instead of opportunities; finding excuses, blaming

V-Day: the term used in World War II for "Victory day". We apply this term to mean the point when we have met a goal – our vision of achievement

V-Day Symbol: a physical object, or still-frame image, that encapsulates all the senses and emotions of reaching your goal in one, instantaneous thought

Warning System: the body/mind reaction to stresses as we approach our habitual limits; our self-preservation alarm; the automatic response to perceived threats; the primary source of suggestions to slow down or give up

Appendix C: Action Plan

Step 1: Set the Target - Goals

Know yourself

> *Think of 5-10 adjectives or statements about yourself. Write them down.*

Dig to the Core

> *Write down five of your core values and desires. Align them with your Mega Goals.*

Commitment

> *Make a commitment to yourself that you will see these goals through. Feel optimism, self-confidence and belief. Make it an oath. Mean it and believe it. Write it down. Say it out loud if it helps: "I commit myself fully to this goal. I can... I will..."*

Mega Goals

> *Imagine you are thinking back on your life on your 90th birthday and remembering the definitive aspects of your years. Choose what you want these memories to be. Construct your legacy.*

> *Write down your long-term Mega Goals. No one can do this for you.*

Part 2: Visualize D-Day

Visualize D-Day

Spend some time thinking about your V-Day. Write it down with as much description and as many senses as possible. Add emotions. Use adjectives. Create a small movie that you can watch in your head telling the story of your day of triumph, with you as the main character.

Create V-Day Symbol

Decide on a V-Day Symbol for your goals. Write it down. Visualize it. Associate it with your efforts.

Part 3: Building Blocks

Subgoals

Write down the Subgoals that will take you towards you ultimate achievement.

Milestones

Write down the logical Milestones that will lead you to your Mega Goals. Create the big picture by numbering them in sequence or creating a chart.

Year 1 Action Plan

Goals:

Month 1 Action Plan

Goals:

Week 1 Action Plan

Goals:

Tasks

Write a list of the common tasks you will perform to reach your goal.

Knowledge

How can you become an expert in the areas surrounding your goal? Write down as many ways as you can think of.

Components/Skills

What skills can you master that will increase your effectiveness? What can you become good at that will help you achieve your goal? Write down as many as you can.

Relaxation Technique

Inhale slowly and deeply through your nose while counting to five, hold the breath for two, then exhale fully for another five count. As you breathe in, use your whole diaphragm and feel your belly button rise as you fill your lungs. Repeat 3-5 times. Next, tense the muscles of you feet and lower legs. Hold for 3 second, and release. Repeat this process along with the slow breathing. Work your way up your body, tensing and relaxing your legs, abdomen, upper body, arms, neck, and face. Continue breathing cycle for 2-3 minutes.

Forge Iron Will

Begin an exercise plan. Write down at least one additional self-control-building technique that you can begin immediately. As always, be specific. Track your progress.

Internal Locus of Control

> *In every challenge you encounter, avoid Vacuum Thinking. Concentrate on what you have within your power to change. Write down an obstacle you currently face, and how you will take personal responsibility and direct problem-solving action in the situation.*

Support Mechanisms

> *Write a list of prospective support mechanisms from your family and social circles. Search for mentors, battle buddies and role models related to your specific goals. Inform them of your goals and ask them to support you. Begin building your support system.*

Contingency Planning

> *Write down the distractions you are most likely to experience during your efforts. Be prepared for them.*

First Steps

> *Write down the First Step you will take towards your goals. Think small. Be specific. Include a time-frame.*

Goal Journal - Treasure what you Measure

> *Start a goal book. Get a notebook or start a Word document to record your goals and log your progress. Update it on a regular basis. Use a calendar if it helps.*

Part 4: Adapt and Conquer

Part A: Mind Over Matter

Awareness

> *Pick a time and place to begin making quiet reflection a part of your schedule. Begin practicing self awareness as soon as possible.*

Second Wind

> *Write down a barrier you want to break through. It can be in exercise, work tasks, habit forming or anywhere you feel like you hit a wall. Incrementally increase effort until you feel yourself get a Second Wind and lunge forward. Realize how much you can do beyond what your Warning System tells you.*

Habit

> *Write down the date which you have begun to alter a certain habit or routine. Count down 30 days and realize that you have the power to make yourself whatever you want to be.*

Warning System

> *Begin noticing and identifying your Warning System in action. Write down a few examples of times your Warning System was initiated over the last week. Did you obey it? Did you need to?*

Fluid Adaptation

> *Build on your Contingency Planning. Add potential changes in conditions and effective adaptations. Build in a couple worst-case scenarios.*

Part B: In the Heat of Battle

F.A.C.E.

1. Face Facts

   Describe objectively the kind and scope of the alteration to circumstances. Make a detailed report of the situation.

2. Accept Situation

   a. New Normal

   Identify some situations of change or distress in your life that you should accept as the "new normal". Reset your expectations. Repeat it to yourself when you feel the Warning System kicking in.

   b. Do It Anyway

   Write down a few situations where you have to overcome resistance to change or discomfort in order to make progress. Admit to the difficulty but decide to "do it anyway".

3. Consider Options

   Write down several alternative strategies you could employ to realize your goals. Weigh the benefits and costs and decide if alteration is advisable.

4. Execute

   Write down your revised First Step. Put rubber to road.

Micro Visualization

Choose a difficult short-term task you must perform. Visually walk through your actions. Think about exactly what you will do and how you will react to your Warning System. Use all your senses as you imagine every aspect of your successful performance.

Micro Goals

Think about the smallest steps you can make towards your goals. Write them down. Be ready to bring your focus closer and closer as progress becomes more difficult.

Percentage to Completion

Write down a few instances when it will be motivating to track your Percentage to Completion. Think of small tasks when progress is very difficult.

Serenity Prayer

List the aspects of your situation that are in your control and out of your control. Resolve to spend your time on the things you can change.

Count your Blessings

List all the positive things that have happened recently. Think of all you have been given, everything going right, all the success you have enjoyed and all the progress you have made. Look forward to a triumphant future.

Avoid Distractions: Physical Reminders

Decide on some physical reminders of your goals that will instantly bring your V-Day image to mind.

Incorporate them into your routine in an unavoidable way.

Avoid Distractions: Checklists

Create a checklist of all near-term duties and responsibilities. Balance others' needs as best you can while leaving room for your own needs – including your goals and dreams.

Rest

If you feel you are at a point of exhaustion, decide on a way to renew your mind and body. Before you take the break, write down exactly when and how you will come back to your goals. Include a new First Step.

Positive Self Talk

Come up with a few personal slogans to boost your mood and increase intensity. Start inserting them into your internal dialogue.

Be Led by Example

Pick a role model of excellence in your area of effort. Begin comparing yourself to that person. Decide how your role model would act and follow that example.

If-Then Statements

Think of 3 habits you want to form or behavior you want to change. Formulate them into If-Then statements. Reread the statements once daily until they become personal rules.

Smile at the Pain

Become aware of your body language. Read a book about it if you get the chance. Become aware of your posture and facial expression. When you feel dark clouds closing in, smile.

Music

Create a playlist of songs that will become a soundtrack to your goals. Start using it to prime your psyche and increase stamina.

Nothing Lasts Forever

Write down a situation that is causing you duress. Envision the future when this has been resolved and things are different. Stay focused on that future and keep working.

Handling Setbacks

1. *Debrief*
2. *Lessons Learned*
3. *Resolutions*
4. *Execute*

Part 5: Celebrate Success

Review Progress Regularly

Set a schedule for analyzing your progress. Mark it on a calendar if it helps. Be consistent.

Debrief and Tweak

When you reach Milestones, do a quick assessment. Review your actions and look for one or two areas to fine-tune. Add them to your future plans.

Look at yourself in the mirror

> *Take 5 minutes and look at yourself in the mirror. What do you see? Are your actions consistent with your beliefs? Are you growing in the right direction? Does the look in your eyes match the thoughts in your mind?*

Reward Yourself

> *Write down some ways you will reward yourself for your efforts, large and small. Link specific rewards to specific actions.*

Display Trophies

> *Plaques, diplomas, pictures, souvenirs – rather than stuff them away in closets, put them on display. Adorn your walls, desk, and mantelpiece – surround yourself with reminders of your accomplishments.*

Self Monitor

> *As you master mental toughness and hit your stride, set a long-term interval for self-monitoring. Make it no longer than a year. Perform a general analysis from top to bottom. Look for fresh insights and ongoing improvements. Celebrate your success.*

Appendix D: Examples

Example 4: Football Scholarship

Self-statements
I like sports, football, exercise, teamwork and competition. I am aggressive and passionate. I am high energy and need physical outlets. Sitting makes me depressed.

Core Desire
Get through college without going into debt or straining parents (financial security), play football on a national stage (glory), be a role model (mentor), make parents proud (appreciation); "You should use your gifts to help others"; "I want to make my parents' life easier"; "I love the feeling of performing under pressure"

Mega Goal
High school freshman – Get a scholarship to play football in college

Timeframe: 5 years

Visualization
First Day of Camp – It was a little frightening to say goodbye to your mom, but it is a relief to be on your own. You got most of your stuff set up in your new dorm room. It still smells like fresh paint. The white walls are very bright, you will want to put up some posters. It's smaller than you thought it would be, but you don't plan on spending much time there anyway. You have an hour until lunch and the first meeting with the whole team, so you call your girlfriend for a quick hello and tighten your cleats. At lunch you try not to eat too much but mix in some complex carbs for energy. College food doesn't seem too bad. Now for the first team meeting. The coaches are more informal than before. They joke with the upperclassmen. Wow, everyone looks huge. After some quick introductions you line up to get equipment.

As you put your new helmet on it finally sets in – you are a college athlete! This is going to be a great four years. They are actually paying for you to play football – a free college degree. What a jump start on life! The pads they give you still smell a little musty and sweaty. It's a good thing Grandma forced you to bring some Febreeze. As you wait for the lift tests, you toss around the ball with some other freshmen you've met. You notice the ball is bigger than what you are used to, a little harder to grip. You do a bench press test, vertical leap and run the 40 yard dash. All the hard hours you spent in the gym pay off – the coaches seem impressed. You feel confident. Some of the kids might be bigger, but you are as strong and fast as anyone in your position. The whistles are a familiar sound and the smell of freshly cut grass make you feel at home...

V-Day Symbol
Football helmet with logo on it; or Jersey

Sub Goals
Become the strongest player at your position by end of sophomore year
Become the fastest player at our position by end of junior year
Get B+ average grade in school every term for next 4 years
Get 1000 SAT score by end of junior year
Build a great highlight film by November of senior year
Lead team in a category: tackles, sacks, receptions, yards rushing, yards passing (depending on position) junior season
Lead conference in a category senior season

Milestones
Start on the junior high team (3 months, Freshman year)
Letter on the high school team (1 year, Sophomore year)
Start on the high school team (2 years, Junior year)
Make All-Conference (2.5 years, end of Junior year)
Make All-State (3 years)
Get scholarship (3.5 years)

Year 1 Action Plan
Goals: Gain 30% strength and speed; attend at least one summer camp; get playing time on high school team; take SAT practice test and score 900+.

Month 1 Action Plan
Goals: Sign up for SAT prep course; decide on the best position for your body type and skill set; establish yourself as a top player at your position; maintain B+ average in all classes.

Week 1 Action Plan
Goals: Begin strength and speed/agility training; document current strength and speed measurements; begin watching sports shows 30 minutes/day; define goals for daily protein intake; study 30 minutes/day for class.

Tasks
Lift weights
Run sprints
Study for class
Practice SAT
Edit highlight film
Practice techniques

Knowledge
Watch SportsCenter, NCAA and college football regularly
Subscribe to Sports Illustrated or other sports magazine
Read about the recruitment process, how it works and what teams are looking for
Study the strategy behind football
Learn cutting-edge weight lifting and nutrition theory

Skills/Components
Become fast
Become strong
Become agile

Learn techniques for your position – go to football summer camps if possible
Leadership
Balance scholastics and athletics – learn time management

Relaxation Training
Complete 10 minutes of relaxation techniques 1x per day for 2 weeks, then as needed to alleviate stress and maintain calm focus

Self-Control Training
Lift weights 3 times per week, do running and agility drills 2 times per week
Study a minimum of 30 minutes a day 4 nights a week

Internal Locus Training
Your high school team is lousy. Concentrate on being the best player at your position in the Conference. Try to raise your teammates who play positions near you. You can't make your team good, but you can personally be a stand-out and raise the level of players around you
You have a coach who is negative and has a sarcastic style. He cuts you down and shows no belief in you or your abilities. Believe in yourself. Decide to achieve despite the doubt your couch, school or anyone else has.

Support Mechanisms
Find a very motivated teammate from the team and start working out together. Someone of similar strength and abilities will be best.
Let your coaches and family know you want to continue playing football into college. Ask for their help. Let your family know you need tons of protein at meals to build muscle.
If you can find an alumnus from your school that played college football, ask him for advice. Meet with him on a regular basis. He will get to relive his youth and you will have someone to give you advice and celebrate with.

First Step
Make an exercise program within the next 3 days, start following it next Monday

Contingency Plans
You have certain abilities on a genetic level. You will probably not be the best at every single aspect of the game. Find your strengths as a player and adjust your playing style to them. Don't try to be everything, carve out your niche.
You are likely to get hurt or sick several times in the coming seasons. When you can't practice, you can still help the team by dissecting film and motivating others, or lifting weights with non-injured muscles.

Goal Journal - Treasure what you Measure
Start a new notebook every January for the upcoming off-season and season. Track your progress in the gym on a daily basis and your other components on a monthly basis. During the season, record your stats from the games and overall performance on a weekly basis.

Awareness Training
Before practice, sit in library and spend 10 minutes in reflection per day. Identify emotions, concerns and sources of stress. Can be combined with relaxation techniques.

Second Wind
When you feel tired during practice, use Positive Self-Talk to push through the pain barrier and finish strong.

Habits
Stretch out after practice and workouts for 10 minutes. Count 30 days

Warning System

Activated before first game, during conditioning during practice, before taking exam in math class, when asking female classmate to homecoming.

Fluid Adaptation
Your team gets behind in a big game. You will need to adapt to the strategy of your opponent.
You are not making strength gains. You will have to change up your lifting routine.
Your coaches start using a new defense. Your position is eliminated. You will have to master a new position.

F.A.C.E.

Face Facts – Your coaches changed defense schemes and your position is eliminated. Went from 4-3 to 3-4 and eliminated defensive end.

Accept Situation – This scheme is the new normal. You will have to find a place in it.

Consider Options – Become a linebacker or a defensive lineman. There is greater need at linebacker and your speed can be showcased.

Execute – Begin practicing linebacker.

Micro Visualization
You are sitting in the locker room before a playoff game. Run through the specific plays you have practiced in your head. Based on the film you studied, imagine the other team's strategy. Imagine yourself taking on blockers, the form you will use as you leverage yourself and make the tackle. Visualize the perfect form tackle, yourself making the right adjustments, getting your base under you as the running back tries to juke... Watch yourself play a perfect game. Feel ready and confident.

Micro Goals

Divide and Conquer
When lifting weights and feeling exhaustion, concentrate on just one more set. Then just 5 more reps, then 3, then 1...

Percentage to Completion
Keep count of the number of games in the season and your percentage to season's end. Each game is a Milestone and needs to be given 100% effort.

Serenity Prayer
You can't change the strategy your coaches employ or the skill of your teammates, but you can eat and sleep well to grow, work out well to be as fast and strong as possible, pay attention to learn as much as possible, and give 100% effort for the best performance every game.

Count Your Blessings
Be glad that you have the ability to play football at a high level, that you can play sports instead of go to work after school, that you have friends and family who support you.

Physical Reminders
Get a mug with the logo of your top choice for college. Use it to drink your orange juice every morning.

Checklist
This week: practice every day at four; meditation for 10 minutes in the library at 3; study for SAT 20 minutes every night; dentist appointment Tuesday; economics quiz on Friday, study one hour Thursday night.

Rest
Football games take a heavy toll. Take a Saturday off and rest from school and sports. Come back rested Sunday evening by watching your game film and studying for class for one hour.

Positive Self Talk
"Bring the heat." Repeat during games, practice, exercise.

Be Led By Example
Ray Lewis, All-Pro linebacker. When the game is going against you or you lost motivation while training, think, "Ray would keep pushing."

If-Then Rules
If it's been three hours, then I will take in some protein.

Smile at the Pain
Whenever your team gets behind, smile. Be excited to turn the tide. Straighten your body language and your self-confidence will bolster your teammates.

Music
Listen to aggressive music before games to build up adrenaline and excitement.

Nothing Lasts Forever
When you are sidelined with an injury, remember that you may be bored and frustrated, but you will have a chance to come back with a vengeance. Prepare yourself mentally to return stronger.

Handling Setbacks

Debriefing – You have a bad game and the other team is able to run the ball over your side successfully.

Lessons Learned – On film you realize you are waiting a second and reading the guard before moving forward and end up getting to the line of scrimmage too late.

Resolutions – Take a step forward as soon as the ball is hiked and read the guard as you are moving forward.

Execute – Make all decisions while moving toward the line of scrimmage, this allows you to close the holes before the ball-carrier gets through.

Review Progress
Track daily workouts and review progress monthly (including one-rep maximum lift) during off season; during season watch your weekly film and analyze performance.

Debrief and Tweak
You have trouble getting off hook blocks. Increase chest strength and practice techniques before practice for 15 minutes with coach.

Look at Yourself in the Mirror
You are getting a free education, your family loves come watching you play, younger players look up to you, and you love the emotional release of the games. Keep going!

Reward Yourself
After every game, spend an hour in the hot tub relaxing with your friends.

Trophies
Team picture, jersey, All-State award, program guide with your name in it.

Self Regulate
Once you are a solidified member of your college team, you have a great work ethic in the gym and are a leader on the field, begin doing a full analysis twice a year – after the season and at the end of spring semester. Celebrate your accomplishment and growth, review the principles of mental toughness, and set some new targets for strength, speed and on-field performance.

Example 5: Weight Loss

Self-statement
I like dressing up, cooking, getting attention/affection and personal time/introversion. I eat too much when I'm bored.

Core Desire
Attractiveness; improve my health to live longer for kids/grandkids (support family), rekindle passion with my spouse (romance, companionship), feel more energetic, improve self image (love myself, don't waste my potential); "Your body is a gift to take care of"; "I want my spouse to love me"

Mega Goal
Middle age accountant – Lose 50 pounds in 8 months and keep it off

Timeframe: Life

Visualization
Final Weigh-in – It's been a long process, with a lot of difficult workouts and a lot of specially-cooked meals, but here we are. What a difference this has made in so many unexpected ways. It's given you something to talk about with a lot of new people at the office, your spouse has started coming to the gym with you and its increased your friendship, you have more energy and feel less stressed. You step on the scale with a slight feeling of nervousness. That's it, you've lost the last pound! You're there. Ready for summer. Slim and trim. Back to your college weight! You put on your bikini and move in front of the mirror. Wow. What a difference. You are amazed at how many years you spent overweight – "I should have done this 10 years ago!" You bust a few moves to show off your new curves and strike a few poses, flexing your biceps for an imaginary camera. You look forward to shopping in the petite section at Macy's as you box up some old clothes to donate...

V-Day Symbol
Bikini or Little black dress; or Scale reading target weight

Milestones
Every 5 pound increment, dress size, suit size or waist measurement inch

Year 1 Action Plan
Goals: Lose 50 pounds and maintain weight/size.

Month 1 Action Plan
Goals: Meet with a nutritionist; lose 5 pounds, hit calorie goals 90% of days.

Week 1 Action Plan
Goals: Start exercise plan; take body measurements and weight; recruit a workout partner; start relaxation and self-regulation training; start goal journal.

Tasks
Exercise
Read to increase knowledge
Cook healthy meals

Knowledge
Learn about proper diet and nutrition
Read about modern exercise science
Subscribe to some living healthy magazines
Read some books about weight loss and nutrition
Clothing and body type – watch shows about what looks good on certain people

Skills/Components
Consult a nutritionist
Learn some basic cooking and food selection
Learn basic science of calories and metabolism
Learn the nutritional facts of common foods

Relaxation Training

Complete 10 minutes of relaxation techniques 1x per day for 2 weeks, then as needed to alleviate stress and maintain calm focus

Self-Control Training

With help of personal trainer, develop 5 day a week workout plan

Use the steps at work at least 1 time every day

Internal Locus Training

You expect others to see the difference in your figure as you lose inches and pounds. If they don't notice, or don't say anything, don't let it bother you. You know the great work you are putting in and you see the results. Do it for yourself and your family.

Support Mechanisms

Try to find a friend or coworker with similar desires to work out with and compare diet notes

Tell your spouse of your intention to lose weight. See if you can get your spouse to set a similar goal, for some co-motivation and bonding

First Step

Get a gym membership next Wednesday and do a 20 minute cardio workout

Contingency Plans

You know there are days when you will be stressed out and over-eat, be around others and follow their poor eating habits, or when you are somewhere that the menu is limited. That's okay, one slip-up won't derail your overall trend. Get back on your healthy diet ASAP and don't dwell on it.

You might not lose the weight as quickly as you hope. Sometimes your body reaches plateaus that you have to break through. When your progress isn't going as fast as you like, concentrate on the fact that you are changing the behaviors you have to, and the rest will come in time. Be patient.

Goal Journal - Treasure what you Measure
Document your workouts daily and do weight and body measurements on a set schedule, every other Saturday. You don't want it to become obsessive or distracting. Set daily and weekly goals for exercise and diet behaviors, and monthly goals for target weight and measurement.

Awareness Training
In shower after workout, spend 10 minutes in reflection per day. Identify emotions, concerns and sources of stress. Can be combined with relaxation techniques.

Second Wind
When you are feeling very hungry and the urge to eat is overwhelming, let yourself eat a half meal. Work this down to just a couple bites, and realize your body can get by with the lower calorie amount.

Habits
Put your shoes away as soon as you take them off. Count 30 days.

Warning System
Activated when hungry between meals, argument with spouse, during exercise, before taking your latest measurements to see progress.

Fluid Adaptation
You are at a dinner party and have no choice in cuisine. Instead you just eat a smaller portion.
Your work schedule changes and you can't go to your normal exercise class. Find the next best class and augment it with some exercise on your own.

F.A.C.E.

Face Facts – You can only ride the elliptical for 30 minutes before you hit a wall of exhaustion.

Accept Situation – You have found your limit, but you will push through anyway.

Consider Options – You could do two workouts to increase calorie expenditure, one morning and one evening, or after 30 minutes on elliptical you could do a 20 minute light walk.

Execute – Staying at the gym and continuing with a walk makes more logistical sense. Increase the times incrementally to burn more calories.

Micro Visualization

As you are driving to the gym, visualize your workout. Plan the exercise you will do, watch yourself performing them with perfect form. Imagine the muscle fatigue you will feel, and watch yourself pushing through it. Feel confident that you will do more than last workout, and look forward to your feeling of accomplishment.

Micro Goals
Divide and Conquer

When your craving for desserts is getting strong and you want to splurge, concentrate on just going one more week without sweets. Then one more day. Then one more meal. Then one more...

Percentage to Completion

Set a goal to burn 300 calories during a workout. As the machine calculates calories burned, think to yourself that you are 10% done, a quarter done, half done, only 10 calories left...

Serenity Prayer

You can't stop yourself from aging, but you can slow the process and age gracefully. You can't make your spouse attracted to you, but you can make yourself attractive. You can't always control the foods served to you, but you can control how much you eat.

Count Your Blessings
You live in a country where obesity is a problem, but starvation would be worse. You have some good friends to support you, you have good enough health to work out, you have a stable job and nice home.

Physical Reminders
You want to lose weight by next summer. Make a picture of the beach the background of your computer.

Checklist
Tomorrow: eat 5 small meals; work out in the evening for 45 minutes; read nutrition book 30 minutes.

Rest
Many diets allow a "cheat day". If you start to feel really tired and low in spirits, let yourself have a full meal of what you are craving and a nice dessert. It may be a little stress relief that will renew your motivation. Plan your next day's exercise and healthy meals, then have a nice meal and enjoy it.

Positive Self Talk
"Inch by inch, day by day." Think this as you work out, during measurements, when eating your healthy meals.

Be Led By Example
Suzanne Summers has become famous for her age-defying health. Read about her and model her attitude and workout techniques.

If-Then Rules

If dessert is offered, then I will have a coffee.

Smile at the Pain
When you are feeling hungry, smile. You know you are getting proper nutrition, so straighten up, feel confident, and keep going.

Music
Play feel-good country music on the way to work. You are improving yourself and should be optimistic about the future.

Nothing Lasts Forever
It's harder to lose weight than to keep it off. Once you hit your target you will be able to eat a little more freely. Think of a year from now when a little treat here and there won't matter and you look great.

Handling Setbacks
Debriefing – You are losing fat, but you are adding too much muscle and your weight isn't budging.

Lessons Learned – You put on muscle easily when you lift weights.

Resolutions – Only do sets of 20+ reps with weights, do twice as many cardio workouts as weightlifting workouts.

Execute – Change your workout schedule to stop building muscle and lose more weight.

Review Progress
Track all your weight loss behaviors and tasks (exercise, learning). Calculate calories and jot them down in your goal book. Have an official weigh-in and measurement of body metrics every two weeks.

Debrief and Tweak

You feel extremely hungry and weak when you wake up. Eat a small, low-glycemic snack right before bed.

Look at Yourself in the Mirror
First of all, you look healthy and attractive! You feel healthy, your relationship is improving and you feel much more in control of your life. Great work!

Reward Yourself
After your bi-weekly progress session, go watch a movie with your spouse.

Trophies
Once you hit your target weight, have a picture taken in your new outfit. Or do before and after photos like the kind you see on T.V. advertisements.

Self Regulate
Once you have maintained your weight successfully for some time, and your exercise and diet routine have become an ingrained habit, review your efforts and analyze your routine on a yearly basis at New Year's.

Example 6: Actress

Self-statements
I like movies, imagination, lives in different ages of history. I have strong emotions. I'm an observer and analytical. I get bored easily. I hate fitting in.

Core Desire
Accomplish something for myself (independence), an outlet to express emotions (engaging all aspects of human existence), captivate and inspire others through roles (education, constant emotional growth); "I don't want to rely on others for everything"; "I need my own identity"; "Art is the highest human endeavor"

Mega Goal
Housewife in New Jersey – Role in Feature Film

Timeframe: 10 years

Visualization
Watching your Movie – You and four of your close friends are in line for popcorn. You are wearing a hooded sweatshirt so you aren't recognized. The popcorn smell, the red carpeting, the giant slurpee, it's all a perfect cliché. It reminds you of your childhood. The excitement builds as you sit and watch the previews. You start to feel some butterflies in your stomach and a grin on your face as the title screen comes up. Then.. there you are, on the big screen! Your friends look over and giggle. What a feeling. How strange yet wonderful. You hear your own voice, you mime the lines as they are being said, you remember how different it looked on set compared with on screen. A feeling of thankfulness overtakes you. You begin to watch for the reactions of the other people in the theater...

V-Day Symbol
Your name in credits; or yourself sitting in make-up chair

Sub Goals
Complete 4 acting classes/year for next 3 years
Act in 1 local theatre performance every year for next 4 years
Act in 1 student film every year for next 5 years
Audition for at least 1 role every month
Get signed with a major agent in the next 6 years

Milestones
Be an extra on set (2 years)
Land a non-speaking role (4 years)
Land a speaking-role (6 years)
Land a supporting role (8 years)

Land a lead role (10 years)

Year 1 Action Plan
Goals: Complete 4 acting classes; perform in one local theatre production; act in one student film; audition for 6 roles

Month 1 Action Plan
Goals: Start one acting class; watch 4 Oscar-nominated movies; read 20 minutes/day book on acting technique.

Week 1 Action Plan
Goals: Make bed every day; start exercise; inform family of your desire to act; research local classes.

Tasks
Attend acting class
Audition for roles
Practice acting techniques
Meet with agents

Knowledge
View all the Oscar contending movies every year
Read books on acting technique and auditioning
Find out what typecast you are and watch movies with those types of characters
Read industry newsletters
Join any acting society or groups in your area

Skills/Components
Auditioning
Voice control
Accents/dialects
Acting technique
Scene study
Character development
Handling rejection

Relaxation Training
Complete 10 minutes of relaxation techniques 1x per day for 2 weeks, then as needed to alleviate stress and maintain calm focus

Self-Control Training
Do circuit training or an exercise class 3 times a week
Make your bed every morning for next 60 days

Internal Locus Training
Acting is a business with lots of rejection. The casting director will have a subjective impression of your audition. You may not be chosen, and you will probably never know why. Put a recorder in your pocket and record the audio of your audition. Evaluate it yourself later. If you did a great job, be proud of it despite what the director chooses.

Support Mechanisms
In your acting classes or groups, find someone who wants to do some scene study and practice together. If you can elicit a veteran actor or teacher to help you and your partner with critical evaluation periodically, even better.
Let your family know you are pursuing acting. Let your spouse know how important this is to you and what it means to you on a level of fulfillment and expression. Invite them to come to your plays and public performances.

First Step
Over the next 5 days, get a list of all the acting seminars and classes in your area

Contingency Plans
Rejection. You know it's a huge part of acting. You will just have to get used to it. Enjoy the acting for its own sake; enjoy the auditions. Have fun, don't count the rejections, but how much you learn each time and how much fun you have.

Goal Journal - Treasure what you Measure
Start a spiral bound notebook. Outline your monthly and yearly goals in it, but also use it to take notes during your classes, while you read, when watching movies, after auditions and productions. Build a body of knowledge as you hit the goals that you are constantly accumulating.

Awareness Training
While folding laundry, spend 10 minutes in reflection per day. Identify emotions, concerns and sources of stress. Can be combined with relaxation techniques.

Second Wind
When memorizing lines you have trouble studying more than 20 minutes at a time. You feel uninspired. Your Warning System tells you its tired. Accept this as the New Normal. Read the scene another 10 minutes anyway. You will hit your Second Wind and your energy levels will increase. Realize you can do more than your body tells you if you just keep pushing.

Habits
Put dishes in the dishwasher instead of the sink. Count 30 days.

Warning System
Activated while memorizing lines, before an audition, before asking a classmate to do scene study with you.

Fluid Adaptation
The role you are auditioning for has a foreign accent. Take classes in accents.
The film you are shooting loses its funding. Try to get some of the completed clips to build a sample of your acting.
Your agent closes shop. Ask him to recommend you to someone else.
Your acting guild goes on strike. Take extra classes and do more student films.

The lighting is so bright you can barely see. Ask the makeup artist if you can get something on your face to reduce glare.

F.A.C.E.
Face Facts – Your agent informs you casting directors see you as a "grandma character".

Accept Situation – You of course don't see yourself as an old woman, but this is the new circumstance that must be adapted to.

Consider Options – You can either change your hair, make-up and dress style and try to get younger roles or start auditioning for "grandma" types of roles.

Execute – Start auditioning for the roles casting directors think you will excel at.

Micro Visualization
Before you go out on an audition, spend 10 minutes visualizing your performance. Relax your breathing. Imagine the casting director telling you to slate and begin. Visualize yourself slating, then going in to character and beginning the scene. Walk through every emotion you will feel and the body language you will portray. Note the pauses you will make and the key parts of the script you will emphasize. See yourself going through the audition calmly, relaxed, completely natural.

Micro Goals
Divide and Conquer
When you have to memorize a script, read it over several times. Then concentrate on just reading over the next 5 scenes. Then the next 2 scenes. Then as your mind grows tired just read the next scene until it is memorized.
When you have experienced several rejections and start to lose hope, decide to just go to two more auditions. Then just

one more audition. Then just one more. You will eventually land a role and your belief will come flooding back.

Percentage to Completion
Keep track of the percentage of an acting class that you have completed, or the percentage of a script you have memorized, or the percentage of a film you have shot.

Serenity Prayer
You can't control what roles you are cast for, but you can prepare for acting in any role by getting the best training and practice possible.

Count Your Blessings
You have enough wealth to pursue creative endeavors, you have a good speaking voice, you are growing everyday and enjoying the whole process.

Physical Reminders
Think of a character that you think would have been perfect for you. Print off a picture of this character and use it as a bookmark in your books.

Checklist
This week: Finish the taxes, attend class Tuesday and Thursday, audition for movie on Friday AM, practice British accent 20 minutes every night, take kids to soccer practice Wednesday and Thursday.

Rest
After you have completed a long play run or are burnt out from auditioning, take two weeks off and do something different. Perhaps you try some scriptwriting of your own, or take a month off and spend your time taking dance lessons or something else that can help your acting resume. Set the specific date that you will begin auditioning again before you take your rest.

Positive Self Talk
"Time to shine." Repeat while studying scenes, memorizing lines, before auditions.

Be Led By Example
Audry Hepburn is the epitome of a great actress for you. Learn about her life, follow her example, live up to her standard when you are feeling stressed.

If-Then Rules
If you begin to feel nervous, take a deep breath and perform as though you are just in your room in front of the mirror.

Smile at the Pain
When you mess up a line, smile. Make a joke out of it and laugh. The more flustered you get, the worse you'll performance will get. Stay confident and show it in your body language.

Music
Listen to some fast dance music on the way to auditions and filming to wake yourself up and get your energy levels high.

Nothing Lasts Forever
If you get stuck in a role that you find tedious, think of it as a stepping stone to better roles. Think of the interesting role you may get next and focus on a great performance to get you there.

Handling Setbacks
Debriefing – You act in your first student film but it is only shown in a class so no one sees it and you can't find student.

Lessons Learned – Make sure you get something out of each film that you can use to build your own personal reel.

Resolutions – Ask director beforehand what the film will be used for, and make sure you get a copy of it with permission to edit pieces out for your personal reel.

Execute – Confirm that you will have access to film for your usage before beginning filming.

Review Progress
Track your activities on a daily basis, noting how many auditions you attend and how many hours you are spending practicing and watching examples of excellent acting. Every month, review your efforts and make sure you are giving enough output to reach your targets.

Debrief and Tweak
You are used to attending classes and performing on stage, and you speak too loudly for movies. Practice reading lines with an audio recorder across the room to adjust your voice to the proper level.

Look at Yourself in the Mirror
You are expanding your skills, exploring different emotions and using every aspect of your creative talents. You are making progress and pursing something artistic all on your own. You feel fulfilled and self-motivated. Awesome!

Reward Yourself
After you audition, sleep in an extra hour the next day and make a leisurely breakfast.

Trophies
Your headshot, play card with your name in the credits, your name on poster of motion picture, your SAG card.

Self Regulate
Once you can go to auditions with complete confidence, you have the ability to relax yourself when needed, you come back quickly from rejections, you feel yourself winning the

respect of fellow actors, begin a schedule of analyzing yourself and your progress three times a year. Get some feedback from your acting coach, look back over the mental toughness techniques to strengthen your resolve, go through your V-Day visualizations, and celebrate the growth you have made as an individual.

Example 7: Sales Leader

Self-statements
I like competition, giving gifts, convincing others, customer service, friendship, parties. I am good at relationship building. I want to minimize stress. I should be more assertive. I am tenacious and have good people skills.

Core Desire
Wealth, being a provider; buy a bigger house to have a bedroom for each of 3 kids (pleasing others), have parents and extended family over for holidays (family time), overcome my introversion and low assertiveness (personal growth), security for myself and my spouse, give to the church (appreciation); "I like winning"; "I get happiness through others"; "You can be whatever you decide to be"

Mega Goal
Insurance salesman – Become top salesman in Division

Timeframe: 10 years

Visualization
Looking at Sales Report – You shorten your usual hour-long lunch because you know the sales figures will be posted at 2. You know you have done well, you've heard the other agents talk and you know you've been landing some of the biggest customers in the division. You feel confident, but you are eager to have the official figures. The fluorescent lights seem especially bright today, and even though it's raining

outside you are looking forward to going for a walk when you get home. You loosen your tie as you wait the last few minutes before the numbers come out. You pick up the Snickers bar that you have been keeping on your desk for this occasion. It feels cool and smooth. Here's the report. Bingo! Top salesperson by 8%! You do a quick calculation of what your bonus will be and text it to your spouse. You think, "Wow, and I'm just getting started. Wait till the referrals start coming in." You tear into the Snickers bar, take a bite and spin yourself around twice in your chair...

V-Day Symbol
Thanksgiving dinner in new house; or Name on Sale Manager business card; or Bonus check at maximum limit

Sub Goals
Double your current customer base in 3 years
Build a solid system for referrals in 1 year
Build a solid system for customer retention in 2 years
Donate 10% of paycheck to church every week
Save 10% of paycheck every week for house down payment
Get to the level that you have no anxiety meeting new potential customers within 6 months

Milestones
Become top salesman in office (4 years)
Become top salesman in region (8 years)
Become top salesman in division (10 years)
Increments of customers: 50, 75, 100, 125, 150, 175 etc.
Increments of dollars month: $10,000, $15,000, $20,000 etc.

Year 1 Action Plan
Goals: Implement referral system; donate 10% of earnings to church; save 10% of paycheck for house; eliminate anxiety towards new customers; 150 new customers; $40,000 more billed monthly.

Month 1 Action Plan

Goals: Ask all current customers for referrals; meet with 40 new potential customers; spend 20 minutes every day reading sales techniques; gain 10 new customers, $3,000 more dollars billed; lower anxiety through practice when meeting new customers; make 200 cold calls.

Week 1 Action Plan
Goals: Read policies and product brochures one hour per day; begin exercise program; identify and approach mentor; meet 10 new potential customers; gain 2 new customers; make 50 cold calls.

Tasks
Practice anxiety lowering techniques
Cold call potential customers
Meet with current customers
Ask for referrals
Write down customer retention system
Read sales techniques
Read product information

Knowledge
Know your product line inside and out, as well as your competition; read all the company brochures
Demographics and geography of your territory of operation, know you market
Insurance rules and regulations - have them memorized
Company's bonus structure, understand the metrics
Read books on sales techniques, listen to audio books on way to work
Learn to spot buying signals, body language cues, and resistance signals
Statistics on costs and probabilities of accidents, be able to explain risk

Skills/Components
Follow-up
Ask for the sale

Customer Referrals
Customer Retention
Cold Calling
Lead Generation
Dress sharp/look professional
Body language reading
Finding a Customer's Latent Needs

Relaxation Training
Complete 10 minutes of relaxation techniques 1x per day for 2 weeks, then as needed to alleviate stress and maintain calm focus

Self-Control Training
Start an exercise program 3-4 days a week or go for an hour long walk every evening
Limit alcohol consumption to 4 drinks a week

Internal Locus Training
When a customer rejects your product, don't take it as a personal failure. All you can do is align the best products with a person's primary needs. You can lead the horse to water, but not make him drink. As long as you present well and clearly explain the risk and product offering, be satisfied.
If your coworkers get jealous at your success and show disdain towards you, don't let it get to you. You will find out who your true friends are, but remain kind, calm and focused on your objective.

Support Mechanisms
Find the best salesperson you know. This could be a senior salesman at work, a friend, or someone you have bought from in the past who impressed you (car salesman, real estate agent, stock broker). If you can't find someone, ask your supervisor for advice. Ask this person to teach you how to become an excellent salesperson.

Ask your friends and family to help you build your customer base. This will be a great base for referrals. Ask them to help you out as a favor, they will probably be glad to help you.

First Step
Be able to write down an outline of every company policy within a month. Begin reading brochures and policy books for 1 hour a day tomorrow.

Contingency Plans
It's easy to get complacent once you get a comfortable income level. It's easy to simply service existing customers and not try to gain any new ones. When you feel yourself going sideways you will need to review your targets and focus on your V-Day Symbol to renew your effort.

Goal Journal - Treasure what you Measure
Get a day planner to keep track of your appointments. You will need to take notes on customers and note follow up and retention dates. Use this to keep track of progress towards your goals. Analyze it once a week to quantify progress towards your next milestone.

Awareness Training
Right after lunch, close your door and spend 10 minutes in reflection per day. Identify emotions, concerns and sources of stress. This can be combined with relaxation techniques.

Second Wind
You get exhausted after 30 cold calls. You decide you want to do 60 calls for the day and you are half-way there. Use Percentage of Completion to count down the calls, and notice that as you go on you pick up steam.

Habits
Floss your teeth twice per day. Count 30 days.

Warning System

Activated while making cold calls, during exercise, during will power practice, while taking a customer's complaint, while reading company policies.

Fluid Adaptation
Your company is purchased and your division is let go. Negotiate the best severance package you can.

Your company changes all of its policies and prices. Relearn them and meet with customers to adjust them to the best new policies.

Your company changes the bonus structure. Adjust your approach to maximize the new structure or start looking for new employer.

F.A.C.E.
Face Facts – Insurance premiums have gone up across the board.

Accept Situation – As frustrating as it is, the sooner you accept the new conditions and deal with it the better.

Consider Options – You could do nothing and let your customers get their higher bills, or meet with them to explain the increases and offer lower coverage if they must keep the same bill structure.

Execute – Begin calling customers and setting up appointments to explain changes and look at alternatives.

Micro Visualization
Before you begin making a batch of sales calls, walk through it in your mind. Hear the phone ringing, visualize the person answering. Walk through the words you will say, the common resistance you will face, and how you will handle each objection. Imagine the call going well and yourself talking in a friendly, confidence, relaxed manner.

Micro Goals

Divide and Conquer

As progress gets difficult, make your new customer goals smaller and smaller. Try to get 50 per months, then 15 per week, then 3 per day. Just take the small next step of calling for the next day's appointments, one at a time. The small tasks will build into great achievements.

Percentage to Completion

If your target is 50 new customers next month, break it into increments of five. Each five new customers is 10% of your goal. Make a chart and color it in 10% at a time to track your progress.

Serenity Prayer

You can't change a company's policies, marketing and prices, but you can work for the company with the best ones. You can't make people buy, but you can present in the best way possible and show them how your products meet their needs in an articulate way. You can't make them like you, but you can look and act professional.

Count Your Blessings

Feel fortunate that you have friends and family that you can invite to holidays, that you have a great spouse and kids to provide for, that you are employed and paying your bills, that you have a great mentor and live in a country full of opportunity.

Physical Reminders

Print off a picture of the dream home you would like to buy. Put it on your bulletin board beside your calendar and use it to remind you of your V-Day visualization and bolster your motivation.

Checklist

Tomorrow: Make 20 cold calls, ask for 10 referrals, 2 new customer meetings in morning, get cat food, go to gym, return phone call of 3 current customers, sign up for sales training course next Saturday.

Rest
Drumming up new leads is the most stressful and difficult part of the industry. You are feeling burned out and your confidence is waning. Take a week off from this and use it to introduce 30 of your current customers to some new policies that they may be interested in. Set a target to get 20 new customers the week you return from the rest. Set down a detailed action plan for that week before you begin contacting current customers for appointments.

Positive Self Talk
"Another day another dollar." Use the phrase to pump yourself up before meetings, cold calls and presentations.

Be Led By Example
Zig Zigler is a very famous author and salesman. He has developed a lot of modern sales techniques. Read his books, see him speak if possible, and try to live up to his standards and practices every day. Think "What would Zig do?"

If-Then Rules
If a customer is upset, then that customer gets my immediate attention.

Smile at the Pain
When a potential customer rejects your presentation, or a customer leaves for a competitor, or you are exhausted from calling or sleepy and exhausted, smile. Finish the day strong and you will enjoy your down time this evening even more.

Music
Get the Rocky IV soundtrack and listen to songs like "Eye of the Tiger" before your difficult cold calls and on the way to presentations.

Nothing Lasts Forever
Right now the majority of your new leads come from cold calling lists. Once you build up a large customer base and perfect your strategy for gathering referrals, you will have many more warm contact leads and spend less time on the phone and more time giving presentations. Think of the long-term dividends your short-term efforts will pay and stay focused.

Handling Setbacks
Debriefing
You had 20 meetings this week and didn't make a single sale.

Lessons Learned
You talk to your mentor, and realize that you did a great job presenting, but you didn't ask the preliminary questions to see what the customer actually needed.

Resolutions
Only present on exactly what the customer needs and is interested in. Ask questions until you identify at least three needs that you can tailor your presentation to.

Execute
Begin all meetings with questions of the customer until you can fit the person's needs to specific products.

Review Progress
The quarterly company sales figures will be your foremost benchmark. But keep daily count of appointments, sales and phone calls made. Analyze your progress towards customer and sales numbers weekly and set your agenda for the next week.

Debrief and Tweak
You are building a huge customer base and having trouble meeting with each customer as often as you would like. Start

writing a monthly newsletter to send to your customers to make a stronger connection and greater loyalty.

Look at Yourself in the Mirror
You see yourself growing and becoming more durable and tenacious than you ever thought possible, you are sharing your success with your church and family, and you are growing in self confidence. Be proud of yourself!

Reward Yourself
Once you set up your target number of appointments for the week, get some take out on the way home and a bottle of wine.

Trophies
Awards for sales leader, pictures of your family at social gatherings, pictures of you with long-term customers.

Self Regulate
Once you have build a substantial customer base, are getting most of your new leads from referrals, feel your Mega Goals as definite and close, have no doubts left that you will succeed, mark on your calendar two times every year that you will meet with your mentor and analyze your progress. Measure whether you are increasing velocity or decreasing, how the industry is changing, what new trends are coming, and enjoy the satisfaction of your hard work paying off.

Example 8: UFC Fighter

Self-statements
I like striving for perfection, learning, physical exhaustion, big risks/big rewards, overcoming trials, pushing limits, self defense. I am competitive and low anxiety. I don't like being at home. I try to give others mutual respect.
Core Desire: Adventure (challenge, learning); to do something that will strain every fiber of my being (being

elite, extraordinary); identity group (friendship, belonging); "Striving to exhaustion makes you feel alive"; "I can be anyone's equal"

Mega Goal
24 year old teacher – Fight in the UFC

Timeframe
By age 35

Visualization
Walking out for the Fight – You can feel your heart pounding heavily. You are forcing your breathing to relax. Slow inhale, slow exhale. The sound of the crowd shakes the whole building, but now that it's your turn to go out it sounds even louder. You think of your friends and family back home watching you on TV. You check your hands and gloves, they feel tight. You repeat to yourself, "Feeling fine, feeling lethal." Your coach indicates it's time to go. You feel a rush of adrenaline as your team lines up behind you at the entrance. You think to yourself, "Win or lose, I made it! I'm here!" Your song starts to play, you step out and see the flood of fans. It's exhilarating; you've never felt so alive. You see the Octagon in front of you and a feeling of grim determination sets in. You can feel the heat from the bright lights and smell sweat...

V-Day Symbol
UFC title belt; or Seeing name on UFC website

Sub Goals
Get a purple belt in Jiu Jitsu (4 years)
Win 5 Muay Thai fights (3 years)
Get enough money from sponsors to fight full time (5 years)

Milestones
Win an amateur MMA fight (2 years)
Win an amateur MMA belt (4 years)

Win a professional MMA fight (5 years)
Win 10 MMA fights (7 years)
Beat a top 10 rated MMA fighter (9 years)
Fight in the UFC (10 years)

Year 1 Action Plan
Goals: Cardio good enough to complete a fight; get two stripes on Jiu Jitsu belt; win a Muay Thai fight and Jiu Jitsu match

Month 1 Action Plan
Goals: Attend four MMA classes per week; watch all fights on TV

Week 1 Action Plan
Goals: Attend one MMA class; practice relaxation techniques

Tasks
Attend classes
Exercise to condition for fights
Contact potential sponsors
Travel to fights
Contact promoters to get fights

Knowledge
Start watching MMA fights, learn the fighters
Read MMA magazines
Read biographies of successful fighters
Play MMA video games
Read books on technique
Understand how the MMA industry works, how to read a contract

Skills/Components
Learn proper exercise and nutrition for MMA
Learn Jiu Jitsu
Learn Wrestling
Learn Boxing

Learn Muay Thai

Relaxation Training
Complete 10 minutes of relaxation techniques 1x per day for 2 weeks, then as needed to alleviate stress and maintain calm focus

Self-Control Training
Develop a conditioning program to get yourself to the cardio levels needed for an MMA fight
Pick one person or thing in your life that is a major annoyance. Determine to not let it bother you. Practice relaxation and emotional control to remain calm.

Internal Locus Training
As you gain notoriety as a fighter, you will start to get publicity as well. There will be articles and blogs dissecting and criticizing everything you do, from your fighting style to your appearance. You will need to be able to zone it out and just concentrate on the tasks in front of you.

Support Mechanisms
Your coaches will become your mentors. Rely on them for advice and development. Your teammates will be workout buddies. Recruit your friends and family as your fans and bring them to your events as a cheering section.

First Step
Research and find the best MMA gym in your area. Join and start taking classes next Monday.

Contingency Plans
This goal will take countless hours of training, coupled with extreme exhaustion and pain. There will be injuries, major and minor. You will need to be prepared to endure the physical punishment and the time sacrifice.

Goal Journal - Treasure what you Measure

Start a goal book. Keep track of your practices and workouts. You will be progressively building volume in work output for both. Keep a log from each practice of the new techniques you have learned and review your progress towards Subgoals and Milestones on a weekly basis.

Awareness Training
As you eat breakfast, spend 10 minutes in reflection per day. Identify emotions, concerns and sources of stress. Can be combined with relaxation techniques.

Second Wind
You get exhausted after 2 rounds of sparring. Count your Blessings and remember how fortunate you are to be pursuing your goal and in great health. Keep pushing and increase your punch count as the third round continues. Realize that you can continue to perform through the muscle fatigue.

Habits
Cover your face with your left hand every time you throw a right hook. Count 30 days.

Warning System
Activated when exhausted during conditioning, when you take a heavy punch during sparring, as you cut weight for a fight, before a fight in the locker room, from bruising and soreness after practice.

Fluid Adaptation
The rules are changes to ban hitting with elbows. Adjust your strategy and posture.
You lose your sponsors due to the economy. Ask friends and associates for a job with a flexible schedule that will still allow you to train. Start teaching at the gym for payment.
You sustain an injury. Attend class and coach other fighters so you can continue to learn.

F.A.C.E.
Face Facts
After a couple fights you realize the other competitors at your weight class are stronger than you.

Accept Situation
This has to be accepted as normal, fighters are getting better every year and you will have to stay ahead of the game.

Consider Options
You can either increase your weight-lifting to get stronger or drop to a lower weight class.

Execute
Lifting more will make you slower and decrease cardio so you decide to move to a lower weight class.

Micro Visualization
Before the fight, on the plane and again in the locker room, visualize the fight. Watch yourself walk out feeling confident and calm, listen to the noise of the crowd. Stay focused and relaxed as you step into the cage. As the fight begins, walk through your game plan. Go through the footwork your will do, the punches you will throw, concentrating on perfect form. Feel what it will be like to connect with your leg kicks, the positions you will take when the fight gets to the floor. Prepare yourself for the fatigue and adrenaline you will feel between rounds. Visualize yourself performing well, sticking to the game plan, wearing your opponent out, catching him with the knockout blow. Look forward to the referee lifting your hand in victory.

Micro Goals
Divide and Conquer
You are doing ten 200 yard sprints for cardio. By number 4 you are exhausted and feel your Warning System telling you

to stop. You do two more sprints. Then two more. Then one more. Then you give everything for the last sprint.

Percentage to Completion
When you are cutting weight, count upwards as you get closer to 100% on weight. You have to lose 12 pounds, so losing three pounds puts you a quarter done, six pounds is halfway there, nine pounds and you only have three pounds to go...

Serenity Prayer
You don't know when or against whom your next fight will be, but you can make yourself the best fighter possible and make yourself an all-around fighter so you are prepared for anyone. You can't control how the judges score the bout, but you can push the pace and fight your fight so that it ends in a knock out or submission so the judges don't get to decide the winner.

Count Your Blessings
Be thankful for your intelligence, for your athleticism, that you have made it this far injury free, that you live near a great MMA gym, that your family supports your venture and you have a chance to make a living doing what you love.

Physical Reminders
Buy a replica or get a picture of the UFC championship belt and put it beside your television. Look at it as you watch fights and visualize yourself fighting in the UFC.

Checklist
This Week: Jiu-jitsu class Tues-Thurs; wrestling practice Wed; boxing Monday; sparring Friday; cardio Wed-Sat; grocery shopping; meet with agent Friday; open savings account; call three potential sponsors; get new shoes for daughter.

Rest

Most fighters take some time to depressurize after fights, even if there are no injuries sustained. The strain of training and cutting weight, as well as the mental drain and adrenaline dump, take their toll. Take a week off, but first tell your coaches you will be back for practice next Monday to work out and review the film.

Positive Self Talk
"Keep swinging." Use this phrase to keep pushing through pain barriers during sparring, bouts, cardio sessions etc.

Be Led By Example
Choose your favorite fighter, such as George St. Pierre. Watch his fights, read about his training habits and when you feel the Warning System taking over, think, "GSP would keep going. GSP wouldn't stop working."

If-Then Rules
If I get hit and dazed, then I will move backwards at an angle.

Smile at the Pain
When you are tired during practice, smile. When you take a big punch, smile. As you recuperate between rounds, smile. It will raise your confidence and intimidate your opponent. The mental aspect of fighting cannot be over-emphasized. And if you do something goofy, laugh at yourself.

Music
Whatever bands get you pumped up, make a mix. Play it during workouts, on the way to practice, while sparring if possible - and definitely before fights.

Nothing Lasts Forever
When you start training, the classes will be basic and fundamental. Remember that you have to walk before you can run. The training six months from now will be much more interesting then it is now. Your early fights will be in

small venues with few fans. You know that as you win fights and move up, you will get into bigger promotions with more fanfare. Look forward to those days when you feel bored with the amateur MMA scene.

Handling Setbacks
Debriefing
You allowed yourself to be put in a Triangle Choke twice during sparring.

Lessons Learned
When in top guard you are susceptible to have yourself pulled off base into Triangle.

Resolutions
Keep your base low and don't let opponent pull you forward.

Execute
Stay low in guard and pull back when you feel the Triangle being attempted.

Review Progress
Track how many workouts you have, how many classes you attend, and your abilities compared with other fighters on your team on a monthly basis. Make a weekly schedule/checklist of what classes you will attend and when you will work out.

Debrief and Tweak
You telegraph your right straight by pulling it back slightly before you punch. Practice 15 minutes per day on the bag throwing the punch directly from your cheek.

Look at Yourself in the Mirror
You are pushing yourself to your limits, you are no longer getting dominated by your teammates, you have a lot of momentum and promoters want you on their cards, you are courageous and relentless, you have a great bunch of

teammates behind you, but you are traveling a lot and miss your family. They support you but you feel like sometimes you let them down. Block off some time after each fight to devote just to them. Keep winning!

Reward Yourself
The day after every sparring session, get a massage.

Trophies
Trophies, medals, your Jiu Jitsu belt, your name on promotional posters.

Self Regulate
Once you feel complete confidence and belief in your abilities, once you have sponsors approaching you, when the thought of slowing down during conditioning no longer enters your mind, start reviewing your progress every year on your birthday as well as after every fight. Sit down with your coaches and look for flaws in your game, work on your fundamental skills, try two new mental toughness methods, come up with some three month and six month goals, and appreciate how far you have come.

Example 9: Marathon

Self-statements
I like feeling healthy, personal time, breaking up monotony, fresh air, stress relief, accomplishment. I am passive. I do well on my own.

Core Desire
Competitive running; build self confidence, do something most people can't do (individuality), give your family an example of how to strive (role modeling), routine (self-discipline); "A healthy body means a healthy mind"; "You need to have some time for yourself every day"; "Always be making progress"

Mega Goal
Complete a marathon and finish in the top 10 every year

Timeframe
3 months – 30 years

Visualization
Finishing race – For the last half mile you've been trying to decide what muscle group is hurting the most, your calves, lower back, lungs or quads. The pain is immense, but you know you are down to the last mile. Finish strong, you are almost there. You think how good it will feel to take a shower, how great your will feel when you wake up the next day, you concentrate on just making it to the next marker, now just to the end of this block, now down to that parked truck. You've kept a great pace, now is the time to seal the deal. Keep pushing, just concentrate on lifting and dropping your feet, perfect rhythm, leaning forward. Don't leave anything behind. You see the finish line ahead and sprint forward. Almost there! You pass another runner who seems to have a limp. You recognize him as last year's runner up. You lengthen your stride and reach across the line. You beat your target time by 40 seconds! You completed a marathon. It worked! How far you have come in a year. Time for a nice long swig of sports drink. For the first time you feel that you are covered with sweat. The drink coats your tongue and you have the strongest craving for sugar of your life. You can feel the blood pooling in your feet as you walk over and congratulate the other runners. Your work out partner crosses the line behind you and you give an approving smile and nod..

V-Day Symbol
Crossing finish line with certain time on clock; or Name in results

Milestones

Run a 3k (1 month)
Run a 3k in under x minutes. (2 months)
Run a 5k (3 months)
Run a 5k in under x minutes (4 months)
Run a 10k (6 months)
Run a 10k in under x minutes (7 months)
Run a half-marathon (9 months)
Run a half-marathon in under x minutes (10 months)
Run a marathon (1 year)
Run a marathon in under x minutes (18 months)
Finish in the top 10 (2 years)
Reducing your run times by 30 second increments for various distances.

Year 1 Action Plan
Goals: Run a full marathon; read biographies of 4 endurance athletes

Month 1 Action Plan
Goals: Join a running club; find running partner; reduce 2 mile time by 60 seconds; study relevant topics 20 minutes per day

Week 1 Action Plan
Goals: Begin exercise and diet plans; begin running and documenting times

Tasks
Read pertinent information
Run and sprint

Knowledge
Begin reading running magazines
Read biographies of endurance athletes
Learn about shoe design and function
Join a running club
Start following world championship marathon running
Study interval training and other advanced techniques

Skills/Components
Learn excellent running form
Learn sports nutrition
Breathing techniques
Pacing strategies

Relaxation Training
Complete 10 minutes of relaxation techniques 1x per day for two weeks, then as needed to alleviate stress and maintain calm focus.

Self-Control Training
Start an exercise program. Begin running three days a week with one day of interval sprints. You will increase frequency and intensity as you progress,
Get a full 8 hours of sleep at least 4 nights a week. Make it the same nights every week. You will need this rest to recuperate from your intense workouts.

Internal Locus Training
When you start out, you will be slower than most of the other runners. It's discouraging to be at the back of the pack. You won't immediately have the respect of the other runners. Concentrate on your own incremental gains, on running your own race, and soon you will be near the front with the leaders.

Support Mechanisms
Find a running partner from your social group or running club. Try to find someone at your level or a little above you, so that you will push one another. If you can find a running coach from a local college who will let you work out with the team, do so. A coach can pass along a lot of useful tips.

First Step
Go to the track tomorrow and complete a one mile run.

Contingency Plans

You know that your favorite time to run is in the evening after work. This is also the time when your spouse and kids want your attention and need your help with household tasks. There are days when you will have to compromise and find other times to work out.

The aching muscle pain and burning lungs is a part of running. You will have to cope with it to succeed.

Plateaus. You know that you will reach a plateau at some point and further gains will be difficult. Rather than get frustrated you will need to be able to adapt and switch things up to renew your body's adaptation process.

Goal Journal - Treasure what you Measure

Make a chart on Excel to track your times on a weekly basis for various distances. Record all workouts during the week and measure them against times from previous weeks. You want to make consistent progress to reach Milestones in targeted timeframes. Track diet plans as well if helpful. Take notes on what mental toughness techniques you are finding most effective as you progress.

Awareness Training

While stretching after a run, spend 10 minutes in reflection per day. Identify emotions, concerns and sources of stress. Can be combined with relaxation techniques.

Second Wind

When you feel exhaustion, concentrate just on maintaining your pace and on good breathing. Use Positive Self Talk and Music to distract you. Once the pain starts to diminish and you get your Second Wind, increase your pace to finish strong.

Habits

Kiss your spouse goodbye every morning. Count 30 days.

Warning System

Activated while running, by soreness/stiffness in the mornings.

Fluid Adaptation
You get a stress fracture and can't run. Do low impact exercise like swimming until healed.
You get stuck in a large pack of runners. Concentrate on form and breathing and save energy to burst out when you get the chance.

F.A.C.E.
Face Facts
There is a heat wave and it will be over 100 degrees during the marathon.

Accept Situation
The race can still be run, but you will need to adjust to the conditions. This is the new normal, and the better you cope with it the more competitive you will be.

Consider Options
You can drop out of the marathon and enter another one next week, or slow your pace a little bit, drink more water and look at this as a variable to exploit to get a higher finishing position.

Execute
Adjust pace and hydration to conditions and as other racers drop back from improper strategy.

Micro Visualization
Before a difficult interval training session, walk through it as you warm up. Visualize yourself sprinting at your maximum level, feel yourself breathing fully and deeply as you rest in-between intervals, concentrate on the perfect form you will have, count the percentage completed as you push out the pain and fatigue and finish strong.

Micro Goals
Divide and Conquer
Instead of thinking of the marathon as a whole, think of it as four short runs – mini-marathons - done back to back. Concentrate on completing each of the short runs to increase concentration and focus.

Percentage to Completion
Count your mini-marathons as your percentage of the whole. Each one is 25% of the entire race. Keep your focus on the next milestone so you don't feel overwhelmed.

Serenity Prayer
You can't change the weather, but you can understand how your body performs and how much water you need. You can't change your genetics, but you can work on your form, nutrition and training techniques to maximize what you have.

Count Your Blessings
Be happy for the nice weather you have to run in, for the warm sunshine and cool breeze, for the beautiful clouds and sweet-smelling flowers, the clean air to breath, for your good health and the feeling of being so alive.

Physical Reminders
Get a dry erase board and put it in your office. Write down your current best times for 3k, 5k, half marathon and marathon as well as the date of the time. Keep it updated with your best times as you beat them.

Checklist
This Week: read nutrition book 20 minutes/day; watch documentary on Lance Armstrong Wed night; run 5k Monday; 10k Wednesday; sprints Friday; carb up two hours before every run; buy ginseng and gingko; eat 150 grams of protein/day; buy new shoes; pay bills; complete Christmas shopping; pick up dry cleaning.

Rest
If you body feels weak even when not exercising, you may be over-doing it. Take 3 or 5 days off and get an extra hour of sleep every night. Plan your workout schedule for next Monday when you come back, and relax.

Positive Self Talk
"No regrets." When your body tells you to stop, tell it no. A few minutes of pain will mean years of satisfaction.

Be Led By Example
An Olympic runner – decide that you want to train as hard as an Olympic marathon runner. Read about them and watch their races. Mimic their workouts and eating habits. What would an Olympian do?

If-Then Rules
If it has been 15 minutes, then I will drink some water. Stay on top of hydration.

Smile at the Pain
Smile periodically as you run. The more it burns, the bigger your smile should be. You don't have to enjoy the pain, but you can enjoy the process of pushing yourself to the limit.

Music
Listen to music while you run. Whatever inspires you, let it motivate and distract you. It won't be there during races, but it will push your workouts and get you in better shape for the races.

Nothing Lasts Forever
When you are in the middle of a marathon and the pain is extreme, remember that an hour from now it will all be over. Pain is temporary, the triumph is lasting. Focus on the end, forget the temporary suffering.

Handling Setbacks
Debriefing
You were on pace to beat your best 10k time and then had an energy crash the last 2 laps.

Lessons Learned
You took in a lot of sugar right before the race. The sugar rush caused an insulin release that took glucose out of your blood stream and robbed your muscles of energy.

Resolutions
Do not eat anything sugary an hour and a half before running.

Execute
Eat a good meal two hours before running and then concentrate on hydration.

Review Progress
Every week, make a game plan for your workouts, target times and distances, and any dietary changes you want to make. Every two weeks, look at your progress and go through the V-Day visualization to stay focused. Change up your playlist to make it fresh.

Debrief and Tweak
You are making good progress in delaying fatigue, but your speed isn't coming along as quickly. Double the number of sprint sessions you are doing every week.

Look at Yourself in the Mirror
You look healthy, you feel healthy. You are enjoying your time outdoors and feel less tense, you look determined and self-motivated, and you have already run further than you ever thought your body was capable of. Fantastic!

Reward Yourself

After your longest distance run every week, have a bowl of ice cream. Your body will need the extra calories to repair.

Trophies
Medals, trophies, your number tag, pictures of you with friends and family after races, official results.

Self Regulate
Once you are able to complete a whole marathon in the top half of the field, your personal slogans/self-talk have become automatic, you are focusing on increasing times instead of just finishing, you notice a change in how you approach all aspects of your life, set up a schedule to evaluate your efforts every three months. Mix up your workouts to confuse your body, look for advances in exercise and nutrition, add some extra elements to your visualization, clarify your core values and desires, and congratulate yourself on your triumph.

Example 10: Debt Reduction

Self-statements
I enjoy cars, travel, clothes, philosophy, hobbies, politics. I like to have power/control. I feel responsibility for others. I get distracted easily.

Core Desire
Financial independence (freedom); allow spouse to relax (be caretaker); start saving for retirement (self-sufficiency), stress reduction (concentrate on higher things in life); "Great things come to those who wait"; "True freedom is from conquering your desires"; "I must take care of my spouse"

Mega Goal
Pay Off $16,000 in Debt then Remain Debt Free

Timeframe
40 years

Visualization
Writing last check on debt – You sign into your bank account to check your balance. Yep, your last paycheck has cleared. You have enough to make the payment. A feeling of relief enters in. You log in to your credit card account and check the balance. "Last payment, here I come!" You fill out the payment information and click "Submit Payment". Done! Debt-free. All paid off. What freedom. The sound of that "click" was like a jailer undoing your chains. You make the announcement to your spouse, share a quick hug, and start to celebrate. The bottle of white wine you have been chilling should be ready. You make a quick toast, take a drink, sit down and exhale. Ahh, done. "I'm going to sleep great tonight."

V-Day Symbol
Credit card statement reading zero

Sub Goals
Only go out to eat once per week
Spend $100/month or less on clothes
Spend $400/month or less on food

Milestones
Consolidate all debt under one lower interest loan (6 months)
Pay off debt in $1,000 increments ($800/month for 20 months)
Save in $500 increments once debt free

Year 1 Action Plan
Goals: Consolidate all debt; hit budget targets and pay-off amounts.

Month 1 Action Plan

Goals: Learn personal finance program
Track all expenses
Spend 3 hours/week studying finance
Lower bills through more competitive services

Week 1 Action Plan
Goals: Know your exact expenses; begin exercise program

Tasks
Budget your bills
Study relevant information
Research and apply for loan
Pay off debt
Save income
Track expenses

Knowledge
Learn exactly what your bills are every month
Make sure you are with the most cost effective company for all recurring bills
Study personal finance and investing books
Take finance seminars if offered locally

Skills/Components
Learn and use a personal finance program like Quickbooks
Understand interest rates and terms of credit
Find ways to make the most money at your present job
Improve your cooking at home

Relaxation Training
Complete 10 minutes of relaxation techniques 1x per day for 2 weeks, then as needed to alleviate stress and maintain calm focus

Self-Control Training
Begin an exercise program, 3 times a week 30-45 minutes
Eat a vegetable in place of french fries for 60 days

Internal Locus Training

You probably feel like you are at the bottom of a well, and blame the credit card company for their exorbitant interest rates. Whether it is just or not doesn't matter, concentrate on what you can change, getting out of debt. Then never let them take advantage of you again.

Support Mechanisms

Since this is going to mean sacrifice for your entire family, you will want to get them on board with what you are doing, and why you need to do it. When they understand the long-term reasons the short-term sacrifices will be easier to swallow.

Find the best financial planner you can, and ask him or her to go through your finances with you. This person can help you invest savings once your debt is paid off, so he or she will be glad to support you to get to that point.

First Step

In the next five days, review your entire expense forecast for the last three months and determine exactly what you are spending in each category

Contingency Plans

Unexpected expenses will come up, it can't be helped. Your family will pressure you to spend more money than is in your budget, and sometimes you will cave. Don't let small set-backs derail your large-scale progress.

Goal Journal - Treasure what you Measure

A personal finance program may be the ideal goal journal to track your goal attainment. You need to track your large expenses as they are made. Analyze your monthly credit card/debit card statement alongside your Subgoals and Milestones.

Awareness Training

While cooking dinner, spend 10 minutes in reflection per day. Identify emotions, concerns and sources of stress. Can be combined with relaxation techniques.

Second Wind
When you really want to spend money on something you know you can't afford, realize Nothing Lasts Forever. Think of the future when you are debt free and have the money to purchase this item. Write it down so you can buy it later. The desire will fade after a day or two.

Habits
Keep all receipts. Count 30 days.

Warning System
Activated when looking at bills, thinking about debt, telling kids they can't buy something they want, during exercise, while studying.

Fluid Adaptation
Your interest rates are raised. Look for a different loan. Try to save a little more each month or and make a little more.
There is an expensive medical emergency. Adjust your targets and keep making progress.
Tax rates are raised. Look for possible tax breaks. Adjust your targets and keep making progress.
You lose your job. Contact creditors and ask for relief.

F.A.C.E.
Face Facts – Interest rate on credit cards are rising by 10%. Your payments will increase substantially.

Accept Situation – It's a harsh reality but it isn't going away. It must be recognized and dealt with. The sooner this is paid off, the sooner you won't have to deal with these cutthroat companies.

Consider Options – You can transfer balance to a new card with a low introductory rate, bundle it under one large loan or take out a home equity loan.

Execute – Try for a home equity loan, then a large loan, and as a last resort a new card. This ranking is done by the relative interest rates of each one.

Micro Visualization
Before you go shopping, visualize yourself making good buying decisions. Imagine yourself comparing prices, putting back unnecessary items and sticking within your budget.

Micro Goals
Divide and Conquer
Concentrate on just paying off the next $1,000. Or concentrate on just keeping your expenses low one week at a time.

Percentage to Completion
Track how much of your debt you have paid off. Every dollar you pay off is one step closer to the goal. Keep track of the payments you make and add them up to see how much you have paid and what percentage of the total has been accomplished.

Serenity Prayer
You don't have control over the price of commodities but you can control how much you consume. You can't control the economy or the tax code but you can do your best at work to get a good salary.

Count Your Blessings
You don't have much money to spend, but you have things that are more important. You have your family, your friends, your health, your car is reliable, your house is new, the weather is nice, your kids are doing well in school, and your team is doing well this season.

Physical Reminders
Plan the first vacation you will take after you pay off your debt. Get a picture of that place and keep it on the inside of your goal book or wherever you track your progress.

Checklist
Tomorrow: buy groceries, spend less than $80; call cell phone company to see if some services can be dropped; read 30 minutes of your personal finance book.

Rest
If it is three weeks into the month and you are out of food and have hit your budget, you will have to go over budget. Make a note of the amount you go over and jot down some ways to lower your expenditure next month.
If you family is getting really low in spirits and you just can't keep saying no, go a little over budget for Christmas gifts or a vacation. Track how much this puts you behind, and write down some ideas how you can make it up in the coming months.

Positive Self Talk
"You'll get there." Repeat this while you are paying bills and making budgets, or when deciding not to buy something.

Be Led By Example
Read about the life of Warren Buffet, legendary investor who came from a normal background and became a billionaire investor, while maintaining his practical, responsible approach to money. Look at his example of how to build wealth conservatively.

If-Then Rules
If there is a generic version of a product, then I will buy it instead.

Smile at the Pain

When you start to feel dismayed because you can't buy something you or your kids want, smile. The mental toughness you are building now will make sure you never have to go into debt again. Have a sense of humor about you lack of spending money to keep the mood light.

Music
Play your favorite party-type music while writing bills and budgeting. Be optimistic about your ability to take control of your life and improve the situation for you and your family. Celebrate the success.

Nothing Lasts Forever
You are taking on more stress now so you can have less stress later. Imagine five years from now when you are saving instead of paying off debt and have extra money to spend as you wish.

Handling Setbacks
Debriefing
You realize that you are paying almost twice what your neighbors are for propane.

Lessons Learned
Check the prices of competitors periodically, even for products and companies you have had for years.

Resolutions
Review all bills and look for savings from switching once every year for every service to take advantage of promotions.

Execute
Call competitors and switch to a less expensive company.

Review Progress

Review recurring bills monthly and build a budget for the next months. Write down your expenses on a daily basis and review them every Wednesday for discretionary items.

Debrief and Tweak
Your expense for your weekly meal at a restaurant is higher than you like. You realize a large chunk of this is from alcohol. Begin going to BYOB restaurants to lower this cost.

Look at Yourself in the Mirror
You are making steady progress, you already feel like you are now climbing a hill instead of sitting in a pit, you see a person who is responsible, reliable and strong, you feel the grip of debt starting to loosen. Great progress!

Reward Yourself
Every time you send in a check to pay down debt, light a fire in the fireplace and relax.

Trophies
Keep the lunchbox you used every day when you couldn't afford eating out for lunch.

Self Regulate
Once you have paid off your debt and starting saving money on a regular basis, you know you are with competitive companies for all your services, you feel low levels of stress and high levels of self-confidence, you have enough internal control not to buy things to "keep up with the Joneses", move to a yearly schedule of budgeting and review. Plan your expenses and income/saving for the upcoming year, build in some monthly tracking mechanisms, note some habits you want to alter, and take satisfaction in your new lifestyle.

Example 11: Family

Self-statements

I like making people laugh, teaching, sharing experiences. I am contemplative and shy in public. I enjoy explaining things. I am sensitive and a little stubborn.

Core Desire: Vicarious accomplishment (teamwork); give your kids opportunities I didn't have; unconditional love (affection); passing down my accumulated knowledge (history); "Children are a gift"; "Love is the most beautiful aspect of living"

Mega Goal

Raise happy and successful kids

Timeframe

Lifetime

Visualization

Being at child's wedding – What a strange feeling, your little one is getting married. You can still remember you own wedding, with your heart full of dreams. You see the same hopes in your child's eyes. You pin on your flower and smell its simple sweetness. This outfit is tight, stiff and hot. It will be a relief to get out of it, but it's just a small sacrifice to make for your child. You think back on all the efforts you have made over the years, all the triumphs and tears you and your family have gone through - sports, school, dentists, clothes shopping, college, broken bones, stitches, diapers, parent-teacher conferences – so many years of so many efforts. But as you sit by the altar, the music plays and see your little one looking so happy, all you can think is, "It was worth it. Totally worth it." There were the first words, the funny things only a child can say, all the years with your best little buddy, keeping you young, challenging you to be a good example, giving and receiving complete trust and love...

V-Day Symbol

Champagne glass for toast; Baby's pacifier; Photo album

Sub Goals
Find a great spouse (No time frame)
Become established and in a career that can support a family (5 years)
Buy a family friendly house in favorable neighborhood (7 years)
Save enough money to help kids make it through college (20 years)
Educate Kids and Instill Values (25 years)

Milestones
Marriage
Birth of First Child
Child Talking
Potty Training
Kindergarten
Losing Teeth
Puberty
High School
College/Empty Nest
Real World/Getting a Job
Get Married
Becoming a Grandparent...

Year 1 Action Plan
Goals: Begin job in intended career; build budget to save for house down payment; go on at least 2 dates every month.

Month 1 Action Plan
Goals: Apply to 3 jobs in your intended career; decide on 5 major traits you want in a spouse and 5 traits you should display.

Week 1 Action Plan
Goals: Research and decide on career; start exercise and will power building programs.

Tasks
Study related topics
Spend time with family
Write in your journal
Research career and neighborhood
Transfer money into savings account

Knowledge
Read parenting books
Study basic child psychology and development
Learn about the pregnancy process
Refresh yourself on school curriculum to help with homework
Read books on relationships

Skills/Components
Basic first aid/medical care
Discipline techniques for parenting

Relaxation Training
Complete 10 minutes of relaxation techniques 1x per day for 2 weeks, then as needed to alleviate stress and maintain calm focus

Self-Control Training
Join a water aerobics class or club sport 3 times per week
Listen to one complete symphony every day without distractions for 60 days

Internal Locus Training
You cannot produce a good spouse. There is no store where you can buy one or shop where you can build one. This goal has no time frame. The aspect that you do have control over is learning what kind of person you are looking for, and making yourself into a person who will be a great spouse and parent. Make yourself marriage material and you will be ready when the opportunity comes.

Support Mechanisms

Single parents know how hard it is to raise a child alone. You will want family and friends you can rely on for support and advice. Find a couple that you look up to and get advice from them on a regular basis. Invite your friends and family to birthday parties, baby showers and holidays to surround your family with good influences and helpful hands.

First Step
Spend a week looking at yourself and decide on a long-term career that will provide security and stability for a family. Decide on a career in one week and break it down into goal components.

Contingency Plans
If you don't find a spouse right away, don't get frustrated or desperate. Concentrate on living a full life with rich experiences that will make you the best parent possible.
If your kids don't see eye-to-eye with your vision for their future, continue to support them but allow them to be individuals.
You will suffer sleep deprivation, monetary deprivation, and go gray worrying. But someday in the distant future your kids will thank you for it.

Goal Journal - Treasure what you Measure
Humans are very difficult creatures to quantify. It's not easy to put numbers to a child to measure progress. You don't want to be overbearing. Get a journal and spend a half hour per week writing about what happened in the life of your family, what new progress was made and what you want to work on during the coming week. It will help you define your objectives and give you a wonderful document of memories to cherish in the future.

Awareness Training
As you brush your teeth and wash your face at night, spend 10 minutes in reflection per day. Identify emotions, concerns

and sources of stress. Can be combined with relaxation techniques.

Second Wind
When your toddler hits the "terrible twos" and you feel like you don't have the energy to continue parenting, make a checklist of the tasks you have to do over the next three days. Use these to stay focused, and realize you have vast energy and patience reserves that you have barely even tapped.

Habits
Take a daily vitamin. Count 30 days.

Warning System
Activated while applying for new job, when waking up early for new job, when going on date.

Fluid Adaptation
You end up as a single parent. Ask your support network for assistance and stay strong for your children.
You are required to move for work. Use it as an opportunity to find the best neighborhood and school district you can find in your new town.
Your child becomes sick. Put your child's health first and adjust everything to this purpose.
Values of society change for the worse. Educate your kids as best you can and show a good example of an alternative lifestyle.

F.A.C.E.
Face Facts
Your child decides to marry someone you don't think is a good match.

Accept Situation

You don't like the situation, but this is your child and you have unconditional love. You are upset, but you will have to love your child anyway and continue to provide support.

Consider Options
You can tell your child your opinion and risk alienation or act happy and accept without reservations the marriage.

Execute
To have no regrets, you tell your child you advise against the decision but accept it and will welcome the new spouse into the family.

Micro Visualization
You are preparing to propose to your significant other. You choose the place, write down the words you want to say, think about how it will feel, how she will react, what facial expressions you will make, and practice it in the mirror or with a friend.

Micro Goals
Divide and Conquer
When you are exhausted because your infant won't sleep, just concentrate on getting through the week, then the day. Every time you feed the child and he or she falls asleep, you are one step closer to the child being old enough to sleep through the night.

Percentage to Completion
You love your kids, but you want to have some freedom back. Every birthday that goes by is closer to your kids being in school and giving you some slack in your schedule. At age three you are halfway to first grade, at age four it's only two more years...

Serenity Prayer
You can't make your child like the things you like, but by exposing him or her to as many experiences as possible, you

increase the likelihood that you find things in common. You can't make your child succeed, but you can give your child good education, good advice and love to lead him or her in the right direction. Provide fertile ground and watch your child grow.

Count Your Blessings
Your child is defiant, but be glad your child doesn't follow the crowd. Your child is energetic, but this is a sign of intelligence. Your child won't stop asking "why?" but this means your child is curious and enthusiastic. Your child tries your patience, but you have the blessing of unconditional love. Your mother-in-law criticizes your parenting, but at least you have a babysitter so you can sleep in once a week.

Physical Reminders
Keep a picture of yourself with your parents beside your bed, so you remember how wonderful parenting can be.

Checklist
Tomorrow: Buy diapers; sanitize the bottles; get babysitter for Saturday; read chapter about the teething phase; deposit check in the bank.

Rest
The biggest challenge in parenting is that it is very difficult to take a break. If you have a spouse or family member that can let you take some time for yourself, use it periodically. Space enough room between children that you can give each one adequate attention while not exhausting yourself.

Positive Self Talk
"Let's go. Let's go." Use this phrase out loud to keep your family motivated. Remember that as a parent, you are not only following examples, but you are an example yourself. Your family will take your attitude and body language as a cue, so be the cheer leader for your little team.

Be Led By Example
Your grandmother always seemed to know what to do. She raised 4 successful children. Ask her for advice, think of what you've seen her do, think what she would say about your parenting, and hold yourself to this example.

If-Then Rules
If I am changing a diaper, then I will use baby powder.

Smile at the Pain
When your child wakes you up at two in the morning, smile. When you are exhausted, worried, or upset, smile. They are growing pains, but they will be great memories at some later date. When you see yourself in the mirror and you look like a sleep deprived zombie, laugh at yourself. Let your spouse laugh at you, too.

Music
Listen to the jazz station or some sing-alongs when you are driving your toddler around in the car - it will give you two something to bop to and share a laugh.

Nothing Lasts Forever
Everything happens in phases for children. One week they are obsessed with Beauty and the Beast, the next it is monster trucks, then Tootsie Rolls. One month its potty training, then brushing teeth, then making friends. Today they are whining about everything, tomorrow you can't get them to sit still. Before you know it, they are taller then you and seem like a ghost in the house. Whatever the stage you are in, realize it won't last. Enjoy it both for its joys and frustrations - it will be gone before you know it.

Handling Setbacks
Debriefing
You took your three year old to the zoo and he was more interested in throwing gravel than watching the bears. You

spent most of your time trying to stay out of other peoples' way.

Lessons Learned
This three year old is not yet interested in animals. Crowds are too stressful.

Resolutions
Don't take your child to public zoos or museums until he is five. Go to parks with play sets instead - places where he can be active instead of educational places that require a longer attention span.

Execute
Next Saturday, spend two hours throwing rocks at the local stream.

Review Progress
Take note of the daily actions you take towards your goal. Review them once per week on the same day and write a synopsis in your journal of the progress that has been made and your short-term goals for the upcoming week. Make a checklist to stay on task.

Debrief and Tweak
Your seven year old is becoming very defiant and disrespectful. Find a privilege your child enjoys such as ice cream after dinner and implement a three strike system in which the child loses the ice cream after three instances of bad behavior. Over time, shorten the strikes down to one.

Look at Yourself in the Mirror
You have a beautiful family, they are not perfect but they love you and you love them. They look up to you and can rely on you. You are able to share the things you enjoy with them and in their eyes the person you see in the mirror is a hero. It's a blessed thing!

Reward Yourself
Your biggest reward is the affection and appreciation of your family, but spend some money to indulge yourself on your birthday every year for the efforts you make.

Trophies
Pictures of your family, drawings your kids make at school, trophies and awards they've won.

Self Regulate
Because parenting is constantly changing as the child goes through development phases, you will have to evolve at the same rate. Continue to learn about children at the development stage of your own kids and journal in your book. Once the kids have gotten to their more independent teenage years, lower your journaling to once every month, and as they enter college and adult life move it to every six months or year. Look at new ways you can inspire them, think of what they might need from you, and be happy at the life that you have shared.

Example 12: Senator

Self-statements
I enjoy public speaking, economics, management. My strengths are swaying opinion, leadership, and assertiveness. My weaknesses are impatience, a temper and being a slow reader.

Core Desire
Public service; feeling of importance (making a difference, use talents); public limelight; bring the plight of local farmers to light (defending the weaker); "I can make the world a better place"; "I should put my talents where they can do the most good"

Mega Goal

40 year old businessman – become Senator

Timeframe
20 years

Visualization
First day in office – Alright, time to get to work. There were a lot of campaign promises and the voters expect progress. Time to roll up the sleeves. But your party leaders want you to spend the first week just acclimating yourself to the office and getting up to speed. That makes sense. You'll need a little time to mentally switch from campaign mode to office mode. After a nice breakfast in the hotel, you make your way to your office. By the time you make it to your new desk you are greeted with, "Good morning, Senator" several times. After a short conversation with your security detail, you sit down and review your day's schedule. Two morning meetings with committee chairs, lunch with your Chief of Staff, an interview for a television station back home, and a meeting with one of the strongest lobbying groups in the country. Before you get to work, you take a minute to sit back in your chair and soak it in. Your office is saturated with beautiful wood trim and shiny brass detailing. Your desk is perfectly stocked with brand new pens with your name on them. You turn the name plate on your desk around, and think to yourself you are one of only 100 people in the country to have this position. What an honor. In the coming days you will meet the most powerful people in the country, be briefed on top secret international affairs, and start trying to get the concerns of your home state constituents on the minds of the nation's most tenacious and competitive leaders. That's quite a responsibility. You get out the list you have made of people you want to call and thank for their support. There's time to get a couple calls in and consolidate some support...

V-Day Symbol

Your name with "Sen." written before it; or Graph of your votes winning election

Sub Goals
Retire from business by selling your company (8 years)
Get business to $5 million in sales (6 years)
Develop a reputation for integrity and public service (5 years)
Participate in 2 charities per year for 5 years
Develop a political platform on key issues (8 years)

Milestones
Grow business sales by $50,000 every quarter for 6 years
Become a State Representative (10 years)
Win primary
Win election
Become Governor (14 years)
Win primary
Win election
Become a Senator (20 years)
Win primary
Win election

Year 1 Action Plan
Goals: Grow business sales by $200,000; attend 80% of political meetings for local party; participate in two charities

Month 1 Action Plan
Goals: Identify two charities to participate in, attend the next meeting; design business growth plan and begin implementation

Week 1 Action Plan
Goals: Watch political show every night; begin exercise program

Tasks
Study relevant political issues

Meet with voters to gain support
Practice public speaking
Introduce yourself to politicians
Implement plans to grow business
Attend charities

Knowledge
Watch political talk shows
Listen to talk radio
Join a debate club
Attend political party meetings
Read biographies of politicians
Take a class in political philosophy/political science

Skills/Components
Public speaking
Networking
Speech writing
Debate

Relaxation Training
Complete 10 minutes of relaxation techniques 1x per day for 2 weeks, then as needed to alleviate stress and maintain calm focus

Self-Control Training
Begin jogging in your neighborhood 3 times a week for 25-45 minutes. Use it as a way to meet people and network as well.
Stop using expletive words completely. Count the number of profanities you use per day and get the number to zero.

Internal Locus Training
As an elected official everything you do will be second-guessed. Practice for this by taking the rebukes and criticisms at work lightly and with humility.
You will have to make hard decisions that only you have to live with. Practice making decisions according to your own

values rather than the opinions of others. You are the one who will have to live with your conscience so make sure that is what guides your actions.

Support Mechanisms

Find a member of your political party who is retired or in a position above you who can be a mentor. The party leaders will be the ones nominating you and supporting you, so find the best people from this group with the most experience and rely on them to bolster your career.

Your friends and family will be the first people you call on for support when you begin a campaign. Start building a base of support by eliciting opinions and showing empathy for their concerns.

First Step

Pick a political talk show and watch it every night starting tomorrow.

Contingency Plans

When you take hard stances on tough issues you will lose some supporters and probably some friends. This is unavoidable. When you maintain integrity you will lose some people but gain some new ones. Be ready to stick to your guns.

Some stances are ones you know will lose. When you are in the minority viewpoint and you know you don't have the votes, concentrate on showing your points as clearly as possible and at least making a clear statement of alternative beliefs.

Goal Journal - Treasure what you Measure

Build a plan to grow your business, break it into increments and implement it. Track your progress on a weekly basis. Involve your employees. Start a log for your political ambitions as well. Keep note of people you can call on for support as you meet them and track the meetings and speeches you give to make sure you are building a base at the proper pace.

Awareness Training
Before you leave in the morning, spend 10 minutes in reflection per day. Identify emotions, concerns and sources of stress. Can be combined with relaxation techniques.

Second Wind
You feel completely exhausted after 90 straight days of campaigning. Ask some people from your support network to accompany you on the campaign trail for a few days to increase your motivation and lower stress. As you continue to build support you get a new rush of optimism and you can push to the finish with renewed strength.

Habits
Stop saying "umm" and other fillers when talking. Count 30 days.

Warning System
Activated before giving speech, during debate with other candidate, when exhausted at end of day, when waking up early to travel.

Fluid Adaptation
The economy impacts your business. Adjust to the new conditions to maximize potential revenue and use it as a campaign platform.
Your platform of issues is unpopular. Find the issues you are most popular with and put them at the forefront of your campaign. Retool.
You lose the election. Get a position within the party or on the staff of a party member until the next election.
Your party loses majority control. Fall back to the issues that you have most popular support with and push these to continue progress.

F.A.C.E.
Face Facts – After a long week of campaigning, at five P.M. on Friday, you are invited to meet an influential person for late dinner that is likely to donate a lot of money.

Accept Situation – Yes, you are exhausted and in no mood to socialize, but do it anyway. Your plans have just changed, make the most of it.

Consider Options – You can try to re-schedule the dinner or change you plans and stay in town a few extra hours to do the dinner tonight.

Execute – This is important. Make the sacrifice, be glad for the opportunity and finish the day strong.

Micro Visualization
You are preparing for a huge speech. Walk through the speech in your head. Breath slowly and feel calm and ready. Visualize the introduction and crowd clapping as you take the podium. Imagine how the crowd will sound and look. Feel yourself begin to speak with confidence, relaxed and at an even pace. Go through the words you will say, the pauses for applause, the gestures and facial expressions you will make. See yourself building enthusiasm in the audience as you deliver a powerful oration.

Micro Goals
Divide and Conquer
You have 10 weeks until Election Day. It's a daunting amount of work. Break it down into weeks. Spend the first four weeks giving as many speeches as possible. Then two more weeks meeting your local organizers and shaking as many hands as possible. Then two more weeks. Then another week. Then push through the final week to victory.

Percentage to Completion

Set a target of 50 public appearances in the next 30 days. Track the percentage to your target. Or count down from 50 to zero – whichever gives you more optimism and motivation.

Serenity Prayer
You can't make everyone agree with you, but you can present your side of the issues in a clear and attractive manner. You can also meet with as many people as possible, to make sure you find every like-minded supporter out there.

Count Your Blessings
You are making a ton of new friends, you are inspiring others, you are meeting some of the most interesting and powerful people in the country, your family and friends are getting a big kick out of your publicity, you have put yourself in the small group of elite people that have run for a national office, you are living in a fascinating, challenging time in history and get to be part of it.

Physical Reminders
Make a list of the top items on your agenda for the first year in office. Tape it inside the cabinet where you keep the mugs, and read it over as you are making your morning coffee. Remember why you are doing this and the difference you can make in others' lives.

Checklist
This Week: listen to talk radio one hour every day; read the memoirs of Ronald Reagan 20 minutes per day; write the outline of your stance on education reform by Wednesday; speech at the rotary club on Thursday; attend daughter's play on Thursday evening; dinner with your spouse on Friday; call the plumber about the leaking sink tomorrow.

Rest
Outside of hospitalization, you do not want to take a single day off during the campaign season. But elected officials often go on "retreats". You will want to reward your staff

and let everyone de-stress. So plan a "retreat" weekend for two weeks after Election Day. Planning rest can serve as a short-term substitute for the rest itself. Let your staff and family know about it.

Positive Self Talk
"Keep moving." Use this phrase to keep your energy levels up during the day, and use it to keep your staff on point as well.

Be Led By Example
What would Ronald Reagan do? How would he respond to this question? What decision would he make?

If-Then Rules
If I have to meet with someone who disagrees with me, then I will stick to small talk and showcase my personality and empathy instead.

Smile at the Pain
Politicians are expected to do a lot of smiling. Carry that over to the moments out of the spotlight. When your staff is frustrated and tension is high, smile. It will lower the stress of everyone around you and smooth the anxiety all around.

Music
Have a theme song for your campaign. Something patriotic that you find inspiring, like "God Bless the U.S.A." or something relevant to your home state. Play it as you go on stage to increase the emotions of yourself and your audience.

Nothing Lasts Forever
The debates are a phase. The primary is a phase. The campaign is a phase. All these phases will end. Think of the time six months from now when you are in office and these concerns are behind you.

Handling Setbacks
Debriefing – You got low poll numbers on the economic part of the debate.

Lessons Learned – People don't care that your tax reforms will be "fair", they care about how it will increase jobs and revenue for the state.

Resolutions – Don't use the word "fair", use the word "effective" to describe your reforms.

Execute – Next debate, you lead with your platform on taxes, and describe the benefits to the voters.

Review Progress
Track your business plans and your personal development on a weekly basis. Set an action plan for the upcoming week every Friday before you leave work, and analyze your overall progress every month. Write down the pertinent issues of the day and your stance towards them. Imagine how you would address them in a speech. Update contacts you have made daily.

Debrief and Tweak
You aren't striking a cord with a certain voter block. Have your staff do some research on this demographic and plan a strategy for the next four weeks.

Look at Yourself in the Mirror
You see a dedicated person of honesty and integrity, you can think of the peoples' lives that you have helped, you see resiliency and firm purpose. You live up to your ideals!

Reward Yourself
At the end of each campaign week, unwind with your spouse at the same restaurant.

Trophies

Your campaign posters, the cufflinks you wore on Election Day, the sign that was on your desk at your business.

Self Regulate

Once you are in office and dealing with the day-to-day functions of a lawmaker, you have become automatic and fluid in dealing with unexpected changes, you have a solid platform of issues and complete comfort public speaking, you can set a schedule of review for every four months. Meet with your staff and political party leaders, review poll numbers, look for techniques to increase your discipline, brush up on some knowledge and skills, and celebrate your achievements to date.

Example 13: Travel

Self-statements

I love learning, other cultures, novelty, relaxation and shared experiences. I am open-minded, curious, and generous. I have a short attention span. I can't stand people who are disloyal.

Core Desire

Sightseeing; knowledge; expand horizons (mental stimulation); bonding experiences/memories with family (sharing joy); "Learning about others teaches us about ourselves"; "Never stop experiencing new things"

Mega Goal

See the World – Visit 5 other continents

Timeframe

20 years

Visualization

Arriving at 5th Continent – The sun is just setting on the horizon, but you are exhausted. The multiple airports and time zone changes have taken their toll, but the smell of street vendors roasting meat awakens your senses. You go to your hotel room to change out of your travel clothes. It's a small room by American standards, but nicely decorated in the local style. It's warm and dry so you open the window and sit down for a minute to rest your feet and enjoy the view. You get out the guidebook and review a few phrases in the local dialect and the history of the town you are in. Of all the places you've visited, this is the trip that you were most excited for. Rich culture, great cuisine, and plenty of sunshine. It's a part of the world that has piqued your curiosity since childhood. The kids are going to ace history class this year...

V-Day Symbol
Passport with country stamps; or Mantel piece with souvenirs and pictures from across the globe

Sub Goals
Learn 2 languages at a conversational level (6 years)
Learn basic world history (3 years)

Milestones
Each continent you visit will be a milestone

Year 1 Action Plan
Goals: Hit budget goals; Learn 1/3 of basic world history; begin language study

Month 1 Action Plan
Goals: Hit budget goals; Read 10 minutes per day relevant topics; plan history classes to take or books to read

Week 1 Action Plan
Goals: Pick top destination; create budget to get to first destination

Tasks

Attend language classes
Read history
Book trips
Save money

Knowledge
Learn about other cultures and cuisines
Read travel tips and how to alleviate jet lag
Read budgeting books to save money for trips
Watch travel shows
Read world news

Skills/Components
Photography skills
Using a travel guide
Geography

Relaxation Training
Complete 10 minutes of relaxation techniques 1x per day for 2 weeks, then as needed to alleviate stress and maintain calm focus

Self-Control Training
Exercise 4 times a week for at least 30 minutes. Include 5 miles of hiking per week.
Set your thermostat no higher than 68 degrees for 60 days during the winter and wear a sweatshirt. You will save some money and get used to layering clothing for foreign weather.

Internal Locus Training
Some places are expensive to visit and will take a long time to save up for. Often your travel mates will not be able to go during the dates that you want to go. When your desired departures are delayed, focus on what you can control which is preparing yourself through history, language and culture studies to make your trip even better when you do arrive.

Support Mechanisms

If you know people who are from, or have visited, the countries you are traveling to, ask them for advice on where to go, what to see, etc. If you can bring your family or friends, prepare for the trip with them to increase enjoyment and excitement.

First Step
In the next week, decide on your top picks for places to visit and rank order them. Build a budget within 10 days that will allow you to visit the first destination.

Contingency Plans
Some places may not live up to expectations. Travel delays are inevitable. Currency fluctuations and airfare prices may delay some trips. An attitude that it's not just the trips but a devotion to learning other cultures will take the sting out of these hiccups.

Goal Journal - Treasure what you Measure
Start a journal book with your top destinations. Use it to track your vacation funds. Keep a scrapbook for photos, postcards and mementos from your trips.

Awareness Training
Go for a short walk every evening and spend 10 minutes in reflection. Identify emotions, concerns and sources of stress. Can be combined with relaxation techniques.

Second Wind
You have only saved a quarter of the money you need for your next trip. You are considering just going to the local beach instead. Look back over your scrapbook from other trips and use these Trophies to inspire you to keep saving. Once you get over 50% of the savings you get in a rhythm and it feels easier.

Habits
Put a napkin on your lap at every meal. Count 30 days.

Warning System
Activated during exercise, in airport line and going through security, when trying to speak to someone in a foreign language, due to jet lag.

Fluid Adaptation
Airfare prices go up and you can't afford your planned trip. If there is another place you wanted to visit that is less expensive, go there instead.
Your luggage is lost. Buy local clothes and infuse your wardrobe with some foreign flare.
You get sick on vacation and can't move much. Watch local TV shows and try cuisine to get the most education out of your time possible.

F.A.C.E.
Face Facts – Your spouse is very worried about visiting a certain South American country with your family due to the recent crime and kidnappings.

Accept Situation – It's true, this is a risk. It's a culture you've wanted to experience for a long time, but you have to accept it as a new rule – this country is too dangerous.

Consider Options – You can cancel the trip and hope things get better in the future, or you can take a train from the airport to one of the neighboring countries.

Execute – "Close enough" is better than nothing. Visit the neighboring country and enjoy a rich culture with less worry.

Micro Visualization
Before you have to meet a tour guide and speak in a foreign language, walk through it in your mind. Practice a few phrases you will need to use, and imagine yourself reading the lips and gestures to gain understanding.

Micro Goals
Divide and Conquer
Concentrate just on the next destination. Don't try to plan five vacations at once, just take them one at a time.

Percentage to Completion
Each continent you visit is 20% of your goal. Continue to add up your achievement. Or count down how many continents you have left. Celebrate getting 25%, 50% and 75% of the savings needed for the next trip to keep the group excited.

Serenity Prayer
You have only marginal control over the cost of the trip and your salary, but you have power over how well prepared you are. Study the culture, cuisine, maps and major attractions so that you will get the most out of your trips.

Count Your Blessings
You are fortunate to live in an age when travel over long distance in a short amount of time is possible, that you have a job flexible enough to give you long vacations, that your kids share your passion for exploring, that your neighbor is willing to watch your house and dog while you are gone, that modern medicine can keep your joints limber enough to maintain an active life.

Physical Reminders
You have started a scrapbook to keep your pictures and mementos from your trips. Put it on display on your coffee table. On the cover, put a map of the next country you are going to visit.

Checklist
This Week: watch Discovery Channel special on your next destination Wednesday; take dog to vet Tuesday; make ethnic dinner Thursday; hike 3 miles Monday; wash the car; renew your passport.

Rest
If you have had some unanticipated expenses this year or your child made the playoffs and the season is going on longer, you may have to delay this year's trip. Use the time to continue your learning about the place. Before you cancel the trip, set the date that you will re-schedule for.

Positive Self Talk
"Here we come." Use it when you are saving money that could be spent on short-term pleasures, when you are staying home while friends go on more frequent, shorter vacations, and when you are dreading the long flight and airport hassles you will have to endure.

Be Led By Example
Dr. Livingstone endured some amazingly harsh and dangerous conditions while exploring uncharted areas of Africa. His curiosity for foreign culture was unstoppable. Be inspired by his sense of adventure to put up with the much less severe conditions of modern travel.

If-Then Rules
If the water is not in a sealed container, then I will not drink it.

Smile at the Pain
When you are delayed at an airport or drowsy from jet lag, smile. Find something amusing and ironic about the situation and share it with the group. Don't let a short moment of frustration send clouds over a wonderful trip.

Music
Get some sample albums of music from the country you are visiting next. Play it while you make dinner and on the way to work to get in the spirit and build enthusiasm.

Nothing Lasts Forever

If the next destination is one that your family wants to visit but you aren't very keen on, look forward to the trip you will take after this one. Enjoy your family enjoying this trip, and soon you will be preparing for a more interesting trip.

Handling Setbacks
Debriefing – You didn't want the hassle of driving a car in a foreign country on this trip, so you went on a cruise instead. But you feel like all you saw was the boat and water; there was not enough time to see the sights properly or taste local cuisine.

Lessons Learned – Some cruises are just joy rides. Make sure you know exactly how much time will be spent at each port and if it is adequate to explore.

Resolutions – Travel by train if a quality cruise is not available.

Execute – Next trip move by train and see things at your own pace.

Review Progress
Assess whether you stayed on target in saving up for your goal at the end of every month. Create a schedule each week for how much time you want to spend learning about your next destination, and review your results from the previous week. Track your exercise, relaxation and will power practice daily with use of a checklist.

Debrief and Tweak
Your camera was not good at taking pictures of wildlife at a distance on the last trip. Invest in a camera with a better telephoto lens.

Look at Yourself in the Mirror
You are a well-traveled, interesting, knowledgeable person. You see a curiosity in your eyes and the smile wrinkles of

someone who has shared a lot of laughs, you look open minded and optimistic. Outstanding!

Reward Yourself
While you are reading your guide book, have a beer. Remember that this is a pastime and should be fun.

Trophies
Your airplane tickets, pictures, postcards, souvenirs, mark a pin on a map of every place you have visited.

Self Regulate
Once you are hitting your savings targets easily every month, watching and reading about your destinations is part of your subconscious routine, you feel 100% commitment, you no longer dread exercise, you can identify your Warning System quickly, you feel very aware of your emotions and can describe them easily, you can loosen your self-monitoring to after every trip. When you get back, take a few days to rest and let the experiences sink in. Then put down a new plan and targets for the next trip, review skills and components, add a couple new mental toughness techniques, and smile at your new trophies.

Example 14: Chef

Self-statements
I need hard work, constant stimulation and a sense of purpose to thrive. I am good at overcoming high stress situations, culinary arts, customer service, entertaining. I am high stress and think quickly. I should relax more. I like being in a groove.

Core Desire
Rewarding Career; inspire curiosity in others (education), manage others (leader), make a good living (security), be

challenged daily (novelty); "Hard work keeps you honest"; "Food should be an intellectual experience"

Mega Goal
Become a gourmet chef managing a 5 star restaurant

Timeframe: 15 years

Visualization
First night as manager – As you finally take off your apron and wash your hands, you notice that they still smell strongly of garlic, onion and thyme. Your fingers seem to have become saturated with it. But that's okay, it's part of the territory. The chopping noise of the knives and the loud voices in the kitchen have died down, and the hiss of the massive grills has been replaced by the soft swoosh of the dish washing machine. It was a long, frantic night. Every Friday night is like that, but this was your first night in charge. With a brand new menu and a very picky clientele. It's the type of pressure you thrive on. And despite the mistakes and complaints that are par for the course, you feel overwhelming satisfaction. It was such a rush! You realize that as chaotic as the evening was, you kept it smooth and focused and won your staff's respect. You absorbed their frustrations and kept them on task better than the previous manager ever could, and you could see that in their attitudes. This all filters down to the dining experience of the customers, and as you debrief with the wait staff the feedback on presentation and menu selection is stellar. Excellent! Not only have you climbed to the top, you display a natural aptitude for making repeat customers with large bills. This will be the first night of many to come. To wind down as you wait for the staff to clean up, you have someone make you the house specialty, crème Brule. As you break through the sugar crust and feel the creamy sweetness coat your tongue, sitting on one of the tables in the corner of the restaurant, you call home to let them know you will be back soon...

V-Day Symbol
Chef's hat; or Menu

Sub Goals
Graduate from a top 5 culinary school (5 years)

Milestones
Head chef at restaurant (10 years)
Manage restaurant (15 years)
Head chef at 5 star restaurant (20 years)
Manage 5 star restaurant (30 years)

Year 1 Action Plan
Goals: Acceptance to culinary school; complete 3 cookbooks.
Work part-time in restaurant at least 1 day per week.

Month 1 Action Plan
Goals: Research culinary schools and receive applications.

Week 1 Action Plan
Goals: Start cooking one recipe from scratch every day and keep notes.

Tasks
Attend class
Develop menus
Gain repeat customers
Study techniques
Practice recipes
Apply to school
Apply to positions

Knowledge
Watch cooking shows
Learn basic agriculture processes
Read cookbooks
Research metals and knives

Study basic chemistry of food
Read some books on nutrition
Read about and sample wines and spirits
Read business regulations and codes of foodservice
Learn kitchen management and restaurant promotion from supervisors

Skills/Components
Various cooking skills
People management
Restaurant marketing
Customer service skills

Relaxation Training
Complete 10 minutes of relaxation techniques 1x per day for 2 weeks, then as needed to alleviate stress and maintain calm focus

Self-Control Training
Circuit training exercise 4 times a week for 20-30 minutes
Drink at least 8 glasses of water per day for 60 days

Internal Locus Training
Taste is a subjective thing. Some people don't like caviar, others love it. If some of your dishes are not accepted it doesn't mean you are a bad chef. You may have followed the recipe to perfection but have an audience that just doesn't like that dish. As long as you made the recipe the way it should be made, don't fault yourself.

Much of a restaurant's success is out of your control. The location, decoration, often even the menu will be dictated to you. You can make sure the recipes are followed correctly and food is made in a timely manner. If you have charge of the wait staff, make sure they are friendly and attentive. If only 10 people eat at the restaurant in a particular evening, just make sure those 10 people have a great experience and be satisfied with your efforts.

Support Mechanisms

If there is a really fine restaurant near you, contact the chef and see if he will let you observe him in action. Offer to volunteer if you have to. Get the exposure to someone at the top of the game. Your teachers at culinary school may be willing to take you under their wing. If you can't find someone high ranking in the industry, just find the most respected person you know and ask him or her to guide you along your career. Even if her/she doesn't have industry knowledge, you will still find it a beneficial relationship.

First Step

In the next 5 days, get three widely-acclaimed cookbooks. Make one meal from scratch every day.

Contingency Plans

A lot of positions in restaurants are a matter of seniority. So no matter how well you do, you will not be able to move up in the ranks. You may be showing great promise and impressing everyone, but if you are behind an established chef you could wait years to move up in position. Sometimes in order to be promoted you will have to move to a new restaurant, and this is a cost-benefit analysis you will have to perform.

Goal Journal - Treasure what you Measure

Start a goal book and use it to keep track of new recipes you use, accumulated knowledge of techniques and weekly progress towards Milestones.

Awareness Training

Go to a coffee shop in the afternoon before work and spend 10 minutes in reflection per day. Identify emotions, concerns and sources of stress. Can be combined with relaxation techniques.

Second Wind

You are managing the kitchen on a very busy evening. Your stress level feels like it has hit a maximum level. Go to the bathroom, splash a little water on your face and do some relaxation techniques. Repeat some personal mantras, accept the situation and decide you will Do It Anyway – you will finish the night. You continue on and within an hour the rush starts to thin out and the kitchen staff catch up on the orders. You realize as long as you stay clear headed your staff will keep producing and the night will be a success. You feel very confident for tomorrow night.

Habits
Say please when you give orders to staff. Count 30 days.

Warning System
Activated while writing menu, when customers complain, when employees complain, when exhausted at end of night, when busy and getting behind.

Fluid Adaptation
On a busy night, you run out of a vital ingredient. You offer customers an alternative item and a free desert that you want to use up.
A vital cook quits without notice. You will have to help out by running his or her station while performing your own tasks as well.
The restaurant you are managing goes out of business. Make a current resume and take the time not spent job hunting to take some extra classes sharpen your skills.

F.A.C.E.
Face Facts – A rival restaurant has started having a lobster special on Fridays and it taking a large amount of your business.

Accept Situation – You don't know how long this special will run, so you must assume it will continue for the foreseeable future and is the new normal, the new status quo for the competitive landscape.

Consider Options – You can have a competing special on Fridays, do nothing, or have your own special on Saturdays.

Execute – They are selling lobster with no profit, it is a loss leader. Don't get into a price war. Let them have the Friday customers, they aren't making a profit and will eventually have to stop the special.

Micro Visualization
Tonight is your first night as head dessert chef. Walk through the evening in your mind. Imagine yourself taking orders, working efficiently and making each plate with precision and flair.

Micro Goals
Divide and Conquer
You are tasked with dicing 80 onions. Count your way to ten, then the next ten, then the next ten, then ten more. Halfway. Ten more. Five more. Five more...

Percentage to Completion
Your culinary classes are eight weeks in length. Each two weeks of effort is 25% achieved. Track your percentage completed to boost performance and increase mental toughness.

Serenity Prayer
You can't change peoples' tastes, but you can try your recipes on many sample groups to fit the local tastes as well as possible. You can't control that people will complain throughout the evening, but you can react with calm so that the stress for your staff is kept as low as possible. You can't make people come to your restaurant, but you can spread word of mouth by giving each diner an extraordinary experience.

Count Your Blessings

You live in a time when exotic ingredients are readily available, there are many great organic farms in your area, you started your career at a young age so you have plenty of time to develop, you have a best friend who is a kind and honest critic of your meals, you are well fed, well clothed and as hectic as the kitchen is, it's better than being bored.

Physical Reminders

Get the menu from a five star restaurant that you would like to manage. Put it on a dry erase board, and beside it start sketching out the menu that you would design. Adjust your menu on this board as you develop it.

Checklist

Tomorrow: go to gym; practice relaxation techniques three times; read chapter 7 of textbook; take out trash; cook lasagna for Uncle Giuseppe for dinner.

Rest

Creativity is a slippery thing. When you are just feeling flat, you may want to spend your time outside of work doing something completely different from culinary arts. Spend a month taking a painting or rock-climbing class. A variety of experience may let loose new creative forces. Before you take the break, get a cookbook or biography and plan how you will start back into the culinary arts after your break. Outline the date and First Step you will take when your painting or rock-climbing class ends.

Positive Self Talk

"The best is yet to come." Use this to keep yourself focused on constantly improving your knowledge and skills, and to look forward to the future during friction-points.

Be Led By Example

What would the Ritz-Carlton chef do? Use the Ritz-Carlton standards to set your own standards.

If-Then Rules
If my alarm goes off, then I will get out of bed.

Smile at the Pain
When you mess up a recipe and a dish does not come out as you wanted, smile. Laugh at the absurdity, as your guests try to be polite while looking at each other quizzically. When the kitchen is backed up and tempers flare, smile. The organized chaos is a beautiful thing.

Music
Listen to Frank Sinatra and similar artists when cooking dinner for your significant other, while relaxing and on the way to work. These romantic genres typify the atmosphere and experience you want to give your patrons.

Nothing Lasts Forever
When you are working on a Tuesday afternoon and bored out of your mind, think that in only four short days the place will be packed and you won't have a spare minute all night. Take the quiet time to prepare the knives and clean the ovens, while building rapport with your fellow cooks.

Handling Setbacks
Debriefing – One of the new side dishes was well received but it took too long to cook and delayed many meals.

Lessons Learned – This side dish takes longer than the meals to make but people love it.

Resolutions – Have a line cook constantly make this side dish throughout the night. Guess as to how much you will need and keep making it so the meals are not delayed.

Execute – Start line cook making batches of the special side dish at beginning of dinner rush and continue throughout the night.

Review Progress
Set a schedule for the week. Plan the recipes you will try, classes you will take, and areas you want to improve at work. Every three months, review your progress in the kitchen responsibilities and performance, look at opportunities and threats to your promotion. Look at your weekly schedules to make sure you are completing the Micro Goals that will move you ahead.

Debrief and Tweak
You tried to help the cook beside you catch up, but got yelled at for leaving your station. Always ask permission in the future before deviating from assigned tasks.

Look at Yourself in the Mirror
You see a person who is vital to the operation of the restaurant, someone who provides an example to the rest of the kitchen, you see a creative face that remains calm under pressure. Brilliant!

Reward Yourself
As you drive home from work at night, put down the windows and enjoy the crisp, cool air. Say a prayer of thanksgiving for the day.

Trophies
The menu you designed, the chef's knife from your first culinary job, your diploma from culinary arts school.

Self Regulate
When you feel the confidence that you can handle anything that might happen in the restaurant, when you don't have to worry about work until you get there, when you can remain calm and think clearly under pressure and you have a great

group of repeat customers, set a schedule to review progress every six months. Review the restaurant's sales and finances, the menu, your current staff, how you have handled difficult moments, your levels of optimism, your satisfaction levels, what techniques have worked and what new ones you could try. Plan improvement for the next six months, commit to continue your growth as a chef and agent of invincible success, and enjoy the position you have attained.

Example 15: Social Network

Self-statements
I like supporting others, commiserating with others, learning from others and having people to rely on. I like to spend time in parties and conversation. I am methodical and even keel. I plan ahead. I don't like change.

Core Desire
Teamwork (shared achievement), safety net (security), bring other people together; "Life is more enjoyable when shared with others"; "Relationships define us more than anything else"

Mega Goal
Have a network of great friends

Timeframe
Life

Visualization
Christmas party – There is your birth family, and there is your chosen family. What a great day it is when you get to have them both in one place! Most of the guests have already arrived despite the snowfall that is slowing down travel across the county. You can smell faint whiffs of the new perfume that you are wearing for the occasion. You look around the room and realize you could write a history of your

life with the people here – friends from various jobs, from the gym, from college and grad school, relatives, people you met through public service, civic groups, clubs, hobbies, restaurants you frequent and stores you patronize. It's like a collage of your life. By staying in touch with them you have inadvertently stayed in touch with your whole past. As you make your way across the room, you exchange compliments and anecdotes with each person. You owe them your greatest successes and you have shared many of their most vivid life moments. So much in common, so many lush memories. What a great sense of connectedness. You get the room quiet and make a toast, as the room chuckles with happy laughter you make eye contact and smile as several of your closest friends...

V-Day Symbol
Picture of you and friends at an event; or Christmas cards from friends on table

Sub Goals
Be a member in 6 clubs/hobby groups (2 years)
Alumni group
Hobby group (wine tasting, sewing, swing dancing, etc.)
Club sport group
Political party
Civic group
Follow a favorite sports team in a fan club setting (6 months)
Become a member of a country club or athletic club (3 years)

Year 1 Action Plan
Goals: Be a regular member in 3 clubs; follow a season of sports team with fan club; find a country club or athletic club you would like to be part of; invite 15 people to your birthday party.

Month 1 Action Plan
Goals: Attend 2 meetings; go to gym regularly; introduce yourself to 8 people.

Week 1 Action Plan
Goals: Research local meetings and build calendar; go to gym 3 times.

Tasks
Attend group meetings
Introduce yourself to others
Ask others questions

Knowledge
Read some basic psychology books/magazines
Know what social groups exist in your area

Skills/Components
Ice-breaking and conversation skills

Relaxation Training
Complete 10 minutes of relaxation techniques 1x per day for 2 weeks, then as needed to alleviate stress and maintain calm focus

Self-Control Training
Join a gym and workout 3 times per week, including at least one day playing a sport (basketball, handball, softball, etc.)
Give at least one compliment to someone else every day. Can be a friend, family member, spouse, coworker – say one nice, complimentary thing every day for 60 days.

Internal Locus Training
You will encounter some people who are not sociable, have no desire for friends, or just plain dislike you for any number of reasons. Some people just will not want to be friendly. This is out of our control. Concentrate on being friendly, displaying yourself in a genuine and approachable manner, and like-minded people will be attracted to you.

Support Mechanisms

In gaining friends you are also building a support mechanism. To learn great social skills, find someone who has them and observe his or her behavior. We encounter these people who are very extraverted and socially at ease. Befriend these people, they will introduce you to others and give you an example of friendliness and openness to follow.

First Step
Over the next week, research what clubs and groups meet in your area. Order your preferences and mark the dates of their next meetings on your calendar.

Contingency Plans
Even your best friends will disappoint you sometimes. We are not able to exhibit perfect empathy for others, so we will suffer disappointments even from people with good intentions. Realize that you are not perfect either and be able to accept the minor faults of others.

Goal Journal - Treasure what you Measure
Keep a personal calendar to track meeting times and important engagements, as well as birthdays and notable dates important to your friends. Keep a contact book or computer file as well with names, addresses and pertinent information about your friends.

Awareness Training
When you do the dishes, spend 10 minutes in reflection per day. Identify emotions, concerns and sources of stress. Can be combined with relaxation techniques.

Second Wind
You are exhausted from work and don't feel like going to tonight's social event. You'd rather just take a nap. But you have committed to this so you will go. When you get there you see some friends and begin talking. Your fatigue is distracted by some very interesting conversation and you meet a couple new people who made it definitely

worthwhile. It was only the matter of getting to the meeting that was tough, once you were there your energy levels rose with the group.

Habits
Remember the first name of everyone you meet and use it. Count 30 days.

Warning System
Activated when meeting strangers, when a stranger is rude to you, when your child gets in trouble at school, when you get a flat tire.

Fluid Adaptation
You are forced to move to a new town. Stay in contact with your friends; visit your old town when you get the chance. See if your friends know anyone where you are moving. Join similar clubs at your new town.
You lose your cell phone and contacts. Send an email out asking people to send you their contact information. Make it an opportunity to reconnect with lost acquaintances.

F.A.C.E.
Face Facts – Your best friend and workout partner is moving away.

Accept Situation – You don't like it but you can't change it. You can't be angry or pout, so accept it and be glad that you have such a great friend to begin with.

Consider Options – You can start working out with someone else, work out solo or join an exercise class.

Execute – None of your current friends work out the way you do, so you join the class for now in hopes you will find a new workout partner.

Micro Visualization

You are driving to a large party. Think of everyone you will know there, and people you are likely to meet. Think of things you will have in common, get some conversation starters in mind and imagine yourself making warm conversation with social ease.

Micro Goals
Divide and Conquer
Going to 20 social events in the next three months feels overwhelming, concentrate just on the events for this week. Then next week. Then next...

Percentage to Completion
You are throwing a Christmas party. Plan out the steps and components you will have to take, and calculate your progress towards the total goal as you progress.

Serenity Prayer
Not everyone will like you or have something in common with you, but the more people you meet, the greater your chances of finding kindred-spirits. You aren't trying to change your personality to be popular, but you can improve your social skills to strengthen your network of friends.

Count Your Blessings
You are good looking, energetic, well-educated, you have a good job and live in a young, vibrant city.

Physical Reminders
Put a small Christmas tree on the table in the hallway to keep your focus on the party you will have. Put pictures of yourself with your friends on your mantelpiece to instill your value in friendship.

Checklist
This Week: dodge ball game Wednesday; alumni dinner Thursday; Tuesday presentation at work, finish it on Monday; read body language book 20 minutes per night.

Rest

Some weeks you don't have the energy levels to meet new people. You are exhausted from parenting or from work, or recovering from an illness. Instead, spend some time with just a couple good friends, call some old friends to catch up, and give your family extra attention. Before you decide not to attend the week's events, mark off the first event next week that you will attend to renew your social activities.

Positive Self Talk

"Live the dream." Utter this phrase to yourself right before you decide to introduce yourself to a stranger, when you are tired and just want to go to bed and before you walk into an event.

Be Led By Example

Your best friend is very social. When you are in new situations and not sure how to act, ask yourself how your friend would act? What would your friend say or do in this situation?

If-Then Rules

If I forget someone's name, I will apologize and ask what it is.

Smile at the Pain

When you feel nervous or awkward, smile. It will make you feel more confident and make you look more approachable.

Music

Whatever lightens your mood, listen to it before going out for drinks, meeting old friends or new friends, while you are getting ready in the bathroom – any time you want to lift your mood and get in a gregarious frame of mind.

Nothing Lasts Forever

If you don't have any plans this Saturday, don't get down. Use the time to relax and meditate. Think of the plans you have for the upcoming week, think of the party you are invited to for the Superbowl, and other future times you will spend with good friends.

Handling Setbacks
Debriefing – You have gone to the same alumni meeting four times and made no friends.

Lessons Learned – This group is made up of much older people and you don't have anything in common with them at this point.

Resolutions – Notice the demographics of groups the first time you attend a meeting, and if they don't seem like you, try a different group.

Execute – Go out to eat with your boxing class on Tuesdays from now on instead.

Review Progress
Keep a calendar for all your social events and a contact book of associates. Update the calendar daily and review it at month's end to gauge progress. Track progress towards your Christmas party in a goal book and review it weekly.

Debrief and Tweak
Your friend's spouse was offended that you did not invite him or her specifically to happy hour. Always remember to invite your friends to bring anyone they'd like.

Look at Yourself in the Mirror
You see a person who is loyal and giving. Your eyes look friendly and open to compromise. You feel like you are part of a life shared with many people and you feel connected. Terrific!

Reward Yourself
When you join a new social group, buy yourself a new outfit to look nice at your first meeting.

Trophies
Membership certificates, photos of friends, gifts from friends.

Self Regulate
At some point your schedule will start to fill up with social engagements. You will be introduced to new people by your friends rather than by yourself, you will feel confident that you have plenty of people to rely on if you need support, and you will be able to easily fill a room with people for a party. You will feel socially at ease in any situation and you can set a schedule to review your progress on a yearly basis. You will still be keeping your events calendar, and once a year you will analyze it to see trends, look over your contacts book and think of the major changes and social events of the last year. You will think of some things you want to change, about yourself and in your social landscape, review the principles of mental toughness and goal attainment, set some new targets, and feel full and joyful for the companionship in your life.

75066186R00148

Made in the USA
Middletown, DE
02 June 2018